Three Steps to Awakening

Also by Larry Rosenberg

Breath by Breath: The Liberating Practice of Insight Meditation
Living in the Light of Death: On the Art of Being Truly Alive

Three Steps to Awakening

A Practice for Bringing
Mindfulness to Life

LARRY ROSENBERG

With Laura Zimmerman

SHAMBHALA
Boston & London
2013

Shambhala Publications, Inc.
Horticultural Hall
300 Massachusetts Avenue
Boston, Massachusetts 02115
www.shambhala.com

9 8 7 6 5 4 3 2 1

First Edition
Printed in the United States of America

⊗ This edition is printed on acid-free paper that meets
the American National Standards Institute z39.48 Standard.
♻ This book is printed on 30% postconsumer recycled paper.
For more information please visit www.shambhala.com.

Distributed in the United States by Random House, Inc.,
and in Canada by Random House of Canada Ltd

Designed by James D. Skatges

Library of Congress Cataloging-in-Publication Data

Rosenberg, Larry.
Three steps to awakening: a practice for bringing mindfulness to life /
Larry Rosenberg with Laura Zimmerman.—First edition.
pages   cm
ISBN 978-1-59030-516-4 (pbk.)
1. Meditation—Buddhism. I. Zimmerman, Laura. II. Title.
BQ5612.R67 2013
294.3'4435—dc23
2013008214

To Mr. J. Krishnamurti.

Even years after his death, the profound impact of J. Krishnamurti and his beautiful teachings on my life as expressed in this book is evident. His unrelenting emphasis on what is remains with me to this day.

Beneficial beyond words!
Thank you, Krishnaji.

From the age of six I had a mania for drawing the form of things. By the time I was fifty I had published an infinity of designs. But all I have produced before the age of seventy is not worth taking into account. At seventy-three, I have learned a little about the real structure of nature, of animals, plants, trees, birds, fishes and insects. In consequence, when I am eighty, I shall have made still more progress. At ninety I shall penetrate the mystery of things; at one hundred I shall certainly have reached a marvelous stage; and when I am one hundred and ten, everything I do, be it a dot or a line, will be alive. I beg those who live as long as I to see if I do not keep my word.

WRITTEN AT THE AGE OF SEVENTY-FIVE BY ME,
ONCE HOKUSAI, TODAY GWAKYO ROJIN,
THE OLD MAN MAD ABOUT DRAWING (1835)

Contents

Acknowledgments

When Krishnamurti died in 1986, I inquired as to who really "got" his teachings. The name of a woman named Vimala Thakar, living in Mount Abu, India came up, again and again. After many exchanges of mail, she accepted my invitation to come to Cambridge and share her immense depth of understanding with all of us. She did that for a number of years before retiring to her home in India. We maintained a correspondence until her death. My original intent was to dedicate this book to her, as well as Krishnamurti, but in her last letter before death, she was firm in declining such an offer. Her writings and many personal exchanges enriched my life and remain a source of inspiration to this day.

Jon Kabat-Zinn has been my dear friend, confidante, and fellow yogi for almost fifty years. Our countless discussions clearly have helped shape these teachings.

Matthew Daniell and Doug Phillips started out as devoted students, and are now close friends and fellow teachers. Our ongoing and intense conversations on Vipassana meditation have enriched my practice and teachings beyond what they can imagine.

Thanissaro Bhikkhu's writing and teaching gives us all the opportunity to share in his wealth of understanding of the Buddha's teaching on the liberating power of mindful breathing. We have had many exchanges on this subject over the years. His careful reading and suggestions about this material were immensely beneficial. We have strong disagreements on many points, but these seem to enrich rather than interfere with our friendship.

Jacalyn Bennett, a cherished friend and student for so many years, constantly urged me, with loving words and financial support, to bring this book to completion. Her encouragement was crucial!

Dennis Humphreys, for many years a devoted student and friend, constantly scolded and badgered me—always with affection and humor—to put what I was teaching into a useful form. Here it is.

Thank you to all the countless yogis at the Cambridge Insight Meditation Center for their questions and reports on meditation practice, and also for transcribing the huge volume of Dharma talks, which provided us with the raw material for this publication.

Joe Shay's generosity was an enormous help every step along the way.

Dave O'Neal. What can I say? This soft-spoken, understated, brilliant gentleman for the third time has informed me that there was really a useful book buried in a mountain of verbiage, and then proceeded to clearly inform me what to do about it. All done with a light touch and humor.

My friend Madeline Drexler, a professional writer and editor, who loves Vipassana meditation and Krishnamurti's teaching, scrutinized the manuscript, giving it the benefit of her expertise. She also made the remembrances of Krishnamurti in the appendix possible.

Laura Zimmerman, a long-term student, highly skilled editor, and also a wonderful friend, shaped a massive amount of Dharma-talk materials into a coherent document, while at the same time maintaining the original voice of these teachings. She made this book possible!

Last but not at all least, gratitude to my wife Galina for her loving support—and for knowing when to tell me to take a break from writing, and when to finish it, for goodness sake!

Three Steps to Awakening

Introduction

To Breathe Is to Be Alive!

Is it possible for a natural, fundamental process, such as breathing in and out, to provide the foundation for a liberating meditation practice?

The Buddha would answer *yes*. He realized that the process of respiration, so often taken for granted, comprises the basis for a method of awakening available to all of you. He called this method *anapanasati*, or "the full awareness of breathing," and enshrined it in the *sutta* of the same name.

Three Steps to Awakening investigates this classic method and presents a threefold approach to it that has evolved for me over forty years of practice, study, and teaching. It is based on my own experience, the teachings of several great masters, and countless exchanges with other dharma teachers and yogis. It is especially indebted to the many students who recognized the value of this particular method—and helped open my eyes to the benefits of sharing it with a wider circle of practitioners.

The teachings in this book differ from classical methods taught in anapanasati only in its three-step structure: whole-body breath awareness, breath-as-anchor, and choiceless awareness. But as will become clear to you, it is not in conflict with the classical methods—far from it! It is a flexible approach that works especially well for people today, offering a series of related awareness practices to move among according to your own skills and understanding. It lays out a clear course for those of you just starting out on the path of mindfulness meditation, one that you can practice with for an entire lifetime. At the same time, it offers an approach for experienced meditators looking to revitalize and refine their practice: after all, even after awakening, the Buddha practiced full awareness of the breath.

Taking a Fresh Look at an Ancient Meditation Practice

In the *Anapanasati Sutta*, the Buddha teaches the sixteen contemplations on breath awareness that comprise his basic meditation instructions. Since the time of the Buddha, this foundational discourse has been taught, studied, interpreted, and reinterpreted. In this book, I encourage you to explore the condensed method, which uses two contemplations rather than the traditional sixteen. The first of these two teaches the practice of breath awareness to calm and steady the mind; in the second, you use the breath as an anchor or good friend to investigate the mind, body, and breath within the same time frame. Without forfeiting the essence of the Buddha's instructions, this condensed method of breath meditation might prove more useful and practical for many contemporary yogis. Just like the traditional full sequence of sixteen contemplations, it can lead you to let go into freedom.

I also introduce a third contemplation, one that is intimately connected to the first two. I call it *choiceless awareness*, although it is also known by many other names, including *pure awareness, open awareness*, and *the method of no method*. In this approach, you pay attention to everything you encounter in your lives, without favoritism or judgment. There is no single focus of attention, not even on the breath. Nothing is discarded. From the seemingly most mundane car ride to the store to the seemingly most powerful insight on the cushion, you are aware of what is happening. Awareness is your approach and your refuge.

The inclusion of this third contemplation is the most unusual element of this book. Certainly, it is the one that might be most surprising to longtime practitioners of breath awareness, and understandably so, for it includes the option to drop the breath as "special" and to take refuge in awareness itself.

Paradoxically, choiceless awareness is the first practice I learned, even before I studied Buddhism! Now, more than forty years of practice and teaching lead me to include it as an essential element in this three-phase method of the full awareness of breathing.

I did not intentionally construct a three-phase approach. Rather, it evolved naturally from many years of practice and from observations of other yogis walking on a similar path. *Three Steps to Awakening* attempts to coherently describe this evolution to yet more yogis who use the beauty of simple breath awareness as a mainstay in their practice—and to all seekers of wisdom and compassion.

BREATH AWARENESS AND THE SPIRIT OF INQUIRY

My own turn to the Buddha's teaching was only possible because the first sutta I heard, the *Kalama Sutta*, differed from everything else I had read or known from my own upbringing. The first chapter of this book takes a look at this sutta, for it is the basis for taking a fresh look at our understanding of the full awareness of breathing. It is the discourse where the Buddha urges his listeners (the Kalamas, a group of seekers in fifth century B.C.E. India) to challenge all teachings given to them—even the Buddha's own.

Have you learned that yet? There's a lot of baloney out there. Years ago, a wonderful Hindu teacher, Swami Chinmayananda, who taught me the Vedanta, said, "The longer the beard, the bigger the fake." And he, himself, had a beard that almost touched the floor!

Yes, the Buddha tells us to take the counsel of the wise. We would be foolish to overlook their immeasurable knowledge and skills. But he also tells us to test the teachings in the fire of our own lives. Listen to them, weigh them, and investigate them. It is for each of us to understand "why do I suffer so much?" "how do I relate to the world around me?" or "what brings joy to life?"

This spirit of inquiry is a touchstone for someone like me, a proud descendent from a long line of skeptics. It is resonant in today's world where so many of us share a wariness of strict orthodoxy in religious and political systems. And without the *Kalama Sutta*, I would not have known the freedom to investigate new approaches to the sutta on the full awareness of breathing, both in my earlier book, *Breath by Breath,* and in this current one.

Retracing Steps

Forty years ago, my first meditation teacher, Jiddhu Krishnamurti, did not teach use of the breath. He practiced and taught choiceless awareness only. I spent several days with him when he visited Boston in the 1960s, and when he was about to return to Europe, I asked him for homework. He said, "Put your own house in order. Start paying attention to how you *actually* live!"

When I heard the word *actually*, it burned right through me. Then he repeated, "How you *actually* live." Not how you think you live, not how you should live, not how your parents told you to live. Moment by moment: How do you walk? Sit? Eat? In other words, nothing is unworthy of attention.

After Krishnamurti's death in 1986, I continued to work with his student, Vimala Thakar, a woman of profound understanding and wisdom. Occasionally, Vimala would make a concession, saying, "OK, follow the breath—but you will not need it as a support for more than a few days! Then just observe what's happening in the mind and body."

From day one, working with Krishnamurti and Vimalaji encouraged a practice of pure awareness and a sincere interest in learning about every aspect of life. They trusted awareness, and the interest in learning that came out of awareness, to do the entire job.

I was powerfully drawn to the utter simplicity and naturalness of just being myself and watching, without judgment, and learning from whatever was observed. To this day, if I had to label myself, I would say I'm a minimalist. I like to find the simplest and most direct way to live, especially in human affairs.

Of course, since it was my first meditation instruction, I did not know any other! In time, though, a gap emerged between my love of pure awareness and my ability to use it effectively. Largely, this was because I lacked a firm foundation in concentration. Years of formal education, the worship of conceptual knowledge, plus ten years of university teaching blocked the gateway to simple, open awareness. Or as my first Buddhist teacher, the Zen master Seung Sahn Sunim, put it: "Too many thinking!"

Knowing that I needed more methods, forms, and teachers than Krishnamurti's approach provided, I attended my first *sesshin* (an intense Zen meditation session)—and from then on, with many twists and turns, I remained within the Buddha's fold. But I never relinquished the practice of pure awareness learned from Krishnamurti and Vimala Thakar. As my first *sesshin* was followed by ten years of intensive, much-loved practice in Korean, Vietnamese, and Japanese Zen, I developed an even deeper and unshakeable love of the simplicity of just seeing.

TEACHINGS ON BREATH AWARENESS

My journey with mindful breathing as my companion "officially" began in 1982, when I was introduced to *vipassana*, or insight meditation, as taught in the Theravadin tradition, mainly in Thailand, Cambodia, Burma, and India. Typically, on the first days of a retreat, teachers encouraged yogis to take up breath awareness as an exclusive object of attention. Its purpose was limited to concentration and to calming the mind. When the mind became steady, it was referred to as *samadhi*. This practice prepared you for vipassana: looking directly into the nature of the entire mind-body process and seeing the lawfulness of the Dharma at work. Here, the term *Dharma* means the natural truth of the universe, expressed in the Buddha's teachings.

I inherited, practiced, and eventually taught that interpretation of breath awareness, until I had the good fortune to meet Bhikhu Vimalo, a German monk who had lived and practiced for many years in both Burma and Thailand. He corrected my limited understanding by teaching me that breath awareness was intended to help create a complete practice that included both samadhi and vipassana. This was news to me! He informed me of a sutta that laid out this teaching in a clear and logical style. "Read it!" he said. And so I discovered the *Anapanasati Sutta*.*

Thanks to Bhikhu Vimalo, I came to understand breath awareness as a complete practice that can take you from calming the mind to knowing the mind-body process, including feelings and mind-states, and finally to insight and liberation.

This practice of breath awareness became so central to my life that I sought out its master practitioners. Due to my good fortune, I worked closely with the great Vietnamese Zen master Thich Nhat Hanh and with the venerated Thai master Ajahn Buddhadasa. Further on, I learned yet more about the *Anapanasati Sutta* from Thanissaro Bhikkhu, a monk in the lineage of Ajahn Lee.

To my fascination and occasional bewilderment, I learned that these three extraordinary teachers read the same sutta, occasionally followed identical translations, yet understood the meaning of the words very differently. To add to the mix, I realized that in my earlier years as a practitioner in Soto Zen, a few teachers taught *shikantaza*, which is a practice of just sitting, breathing, and awareness. Though no reference was made to the *Anapanasati Sutta*, looking back, I realized that full breath awareness existed in Zen, too, but it was not called by that name.

Each teacher understood anapanasati as an approach to liberation, yet taught this sutta in distinctly different ways. And each interpretation was authentic, useful, and effective—"correct."

Over time, I came to believe that even if the Buddha were to come back, he might not offer a "one-way only" interpretation, because he was a practitioner of skillful means: he varied his approach

---

* Majjhima Nikaya 118.

and words, depending on the student. The depth of the sutta's "aliveness" and pliability became unmistakable to me. Its organic nature makes it relevant for the problems we face in our complex world, just as it did for the Buddha's world more than twenty-five hundred years ago. Simultaneously, I realized that I had practiced the same number of years as many of the teachers of these suttas. These insights led me to consider putting in my own "two cents," and so I did—first in *Breath by Breath,* published in 1998, and now again, in *Three Steps to Awakening.*

The Condensed Method of Full Awareness of Breathing

The condensed method of two contemplations, rather than sixteen, sounds new to most of us. But I didn't invent it! Years ago, despite his method of instructing students to move sequentially through the entire sutta, Ajahn Buddhadasa strongly suggested that a contemporary yogi without sufficient time to carefully progress through each of the sixteen contemplations might benefit from the condensed method—without losing the essence of the teachings. The great Thai lay meditation teacher Upasika Kee also offers in her writings and discourses a guide to the condensed practice of breath meditation. "If you can become skilled at looking and knowing in this way," she writes, "you'll be struck with the inconstancy, stressfulness, and not-selfness of your 'self,' and you'll meet with the genuine Dharma."

The earlier work *Breath by Breath* devoted only a brief chapter to these two teachers' approaches to the condensed method. At that time, I perceived its benefits, but only partially. Fifteen years later, I am a convert—but it is my own experience and that of many yogis that has convinced me of the immeasurable value of the condensed methods. Clearly, the shorter method is in better synch with our lives as lay practitioners in a quickly spinning world, for it offers the core of the entire *Anapanasati Sutta* in a far more direct and economical manner. Also, because I live in Cambridge, Massachusetts, an academic and professional hub, I've seen many yogis approach the sixteen contemplations as if they were working on a PhD thesis, one that required extensive comparative analyses. This purely intellectual approach, useful for scholars, often impedes the liberating potential of the yogi's actual meditation practice.

Now and then, I encounter yogis drawn to move through all sixteen in ways that genuinely reduce their suffering. Of course, I encourage them to pursue this method—and I encourage you to take the time to read the full sutta, and to pay attention to your own response. As you will hear me say throughout, each yogi responds to a particular approach in his or her own way. For both teacher and student, the choice of methods remains "skillful means." No one size fits all.

But please do not think of the condensed method as "vipassana lite"! As you practice with it on the cushion, at home, or in the office, you will see that I am showing you yet another way to use breath awareness to accomplish what the Buddha taught: how to live skillfully in a world of impermanence and change. The breath accompanies you the full length of life's road: you learn about the body, feelings, mental formations, the mind itself, and, finally, the lawfulness of impermanence and emptiness of a substantial self. The condensed method of breathing is a practice of letting go into freedom.

FULL CIRCLE BACK TO BEGINNINGS: CHOICELESS AWARENESS

Over the course of forty years, my path led from Krishnamurti and choiceless awareness to a decade of Zen to thirty years of insight practice and breath awareness. Paradoxically, as my insight practice evolved, breath awareness became the springboard for not needing the breath as a targeted object of attention.

This was not a deliberate movement on my part. Without effort or conscious intention, awareness itself—my initial practice—emerged more strengthened and intact than ever. Apparently, the methods I'd learned over many years—koans, mantras, yoga, *pranayama*, mental noting, and, of course, breath awareness—helped develop a foundation to more skillfully practice "the method of no method"!

I want to emphasize the noncontrived nature of this process. Strange as it may sound, it simply happened: the breath faded as a prominent component of my practice. Quite naturally, when I sat down to meditate, I loved having nothing to do but sit and learn. Put another way, it was as if the breath itself told me (with a slight Brooklyn accent), "Hey, Larry, look, I've carried you this far. I'm always here for you. But right now, your awareness is not too bad. Actually, you're able to just be aware. You no longer have to start practice by intentionally using the breath as an anchor or friend."

I had traveled full circle back to where I had begun meditation: the practice of choiceless awareness. By this time, though, I had experienced lengthy and intensive practice in Asia and the West, on the cushion and in daily life. I was equipped to make awareness my home.

Until now, I didn't keep track of these gradual shifts in my meditative journey. I did not articulate them to others or even to myself. I continued to teach anapanasati, but my passion was choiceless awareness. As a result, I neglected or slighted the emphasis previously placed on the primacy of the breath.

Fortunately, many longtime students perceived the change in my teaching style. Several started to badger me with the question, Why have you backed off from teaching breath awareness? They pointed out that though I welcomed yogi-initiated discussions of the method, I did not put full energy into it. They also observed that many students attempted to practice pure awareness, but their questions showed they weren't ready for it.

In essence, these observant, longtime yogis asked, Why completely drop a tried-and-true stage of practice that had benefited countless yogis? As I listened, they reminded me that they had started with me, years ago, using anapanasati as a full-fledged practice. They intimately knew the benefits of learning this approach. In fact, some of their practices, too, had unfolded quite naturally, without effort or intent, into awareness in and of itself. They used breath awareness from time to time but no longer in the singular and directed manner of their earlier practice with anapanasati.

As had been true for me, too, breath awareness ushered these students to the point where they could just be aware. Period. Listening to them, one image that came to mind was that of the pole-vaulter. At first, the athlete needs a pole to propel him or herself to a great height. At a certain point, the athlete has to release the pole and just jump.

To varying degrees, this happens to many meditators. Of course, for many others, it does not. From the Buddha's time up until today, some yogis have sustained the practice of breath awareness and remained happy with it, deepening their wisdom and compassion. Clearly, it is not an inferior method. Your individual temperament, degree of practice experience, access to teachers, and a host of other factors determine the particular dharma path you follow. All lead to the same place: to diminished suffering in your life and in the world.

WHAT NOW?

Nothing that follows in this book claims to be the new, improved way to meditate—or the exclusively correct one. Far from it! All I can say with total certainty is that I know the benefits of these teachings for myself, and for many other yogis, each of us utilizing them according to our nature and understanding.

I suggest that you read the book in its entirety before deciding whether to use these teachings. After you read and reflect on the text, if you are interested, start with the first method, and move on from there. Though not intended to prescribe a fixed progression, the sequence of methods do provide a framework and foundation from which to launch a fruitful meditation practice.

Most experienced yogis already know the value of relaxed, alert, exclusive attention to breath sensations. What might be new in this first method is encouragement to attend to wherever the breath is most vivid, rather than on the more frequently designated areas of the nose, chest, or abdomen. Try it and see!

For beginners and longtime yogis alike, whole-body breath awareness can bring the mind to a calm steadiness, making it fit to investigate the entire mind-body process. It ushers you to the second method: breath-as-anchor. Here, whole-body breath awareness and *everything* else that is other than the breath—feelings, sensations, emotions, mental states (including silence)—are viewed within the same time frame. Attention to the breath and all else is synchronized and simultaneous, even as you learn to look at powerful, highly charged emotions such as anxiety or anger.

As you continue these practices, often alternating between the first two methods, you may naturally move to choiceless awareness. Here, openness to the agenda set by Life is simply and naturally observed. Awareness becomes a way of life. You look and listen to what is happening internally and externally, learning from everything you observe.

Now let me qualify an earlier remark: though I recommend going from one approach to the next to the next, there is no "best" or mandatory progression. So, too, your movement through these three steps may be intentional (one to two to three) or may be a natural unfolding of your practice. Some may read this text and find a readiness and interest in choiceless awareness. Fine! Jump in. You will still be sensitive to breathing, though no longer with the breath as an "official" object of awareness. Some will cultivate an ease of moving in and out of all three methods; others will use the breath exclusively, and then drop it. For some, the breath may be the vehicle to bring you to cessation of suffering. Still others will practice choiceless awareness as the most direct path to freedom.

No solid wall separates these three methods. What exists between them is merely a permeable membrane. Above all, I urge you to investigate, stay alert and fresh, and let intelligence and awareness guide you. These qualities will help you align a particular approach with your individual conditions and experiences, which will be endlessly in flux.

Whatever approach you follow, where will you practice it? As you will hear me say, over and over: everywhere! In my own case,

I was taught from day one to practice awareness in nature, at a desk, in a meditation hall, or at home, mopping the floor. This understanding of practice has only deepened over the years. Formal meditation practice and what we call "the rest of life" are inseparable.

The chapters on daily life and relationships appear last in the order of this book—a perfect example of how the sequencing of the text does not express a hierarchy of values. Awareness in relationships with other human beings might be the most imperative, challenging, and unexplored element of practice for contemporary yogis. It is here that our practice will most profoundly benefit or harm ourselves, the people whom we love, and the entire world in which we live.

Learning How to Live

Each of you experiences lawful mental and bodily states, and each knows sorrow and happiness. What's radical about the Buddha's teaching is that it offers you a new way to relate to this shared humanity. As you practice anapanasati and choiceless awareness, you investigate the quality of your life and see that you possess the key to your happiness and suffering.

The Buddha's teachings are a form of training and education—what I have come to call the skill of "learning how to live." Of course, countless circumstances are beyond your control. But as you practice, day after day, year after year, you come to know that the sorrows in the world can be observed and relinquished because they are mind-made. This is where contemplative practices yield their greatest fruit.

Vipassana meditation, using the process of natural breathing, is a wisdom practice. You learn to live with "the two wings of one bird": wisdom and compassion. Isn't this why you put so much energy and effort into approaches such as full awareness of breathing or choiceless awareness? In time, they help you commit less harm to yourself, the people around you, and the world you live in. This is my understanding of waking up.

Three Steps to Awakening reflects the teachings I've been fortunate to learn from others and the experiences of eight decades of life. I'm grateful to someone called the Buddha and to people who have kept the teachings alive for thousands of years. I was fortunate to receive it from some of them and in turn, to share what I've learned with you.

Please investigate whether these approaches help you, too, live with greater wisdom and compassion. As you practice, moment by moment, you are learning how to live. This learning will go on for as long as you go on.

Kalama Sutta

The Right to Question

THE PRACTICE OF THE DHARMA is learning how to live, and it is both a joyful and challenging path. It asks that you open your mind to take a fresh look at your views and opinions, and to accept nothing on faith alone. As you practice, you will be encouraged to investigate your most cherished convictions, even those you may have about the Dharma itself. Happily, this can be a never-ending journey of self-discovery into every aspect of your life.

Of all the teachings of the Buddha, the *Kalama Sutta* is one of my favorites precisely because it encourages this profound interest in the Dharma. The Kalamas were a group of people living in India at the time of the Buddha, and they questioned him about how to recognize wise and authentic teachings. Indeed, if Buddhism were not infused with the spirit of this sutta—a spirit of questioning and testing—I'm quite sure I would not have this meditative practice today.

The teachings in this book are offered in the spirit of the *Kalama Sutta*. Here, I will share my understanding of breath awareness and of choiceless awareness in formal meditation practice and also in daily life, where I'll stress the urgency of bringing the practice into our relationships with one another. Each of these approaches have been tested in the laboratory of my own life and the lives of countless other students and yogis.

From there, it's up to you. "The proof of the pudding is in the eating." You have to bite into the pudding, chew it, and taste it. This familiar adage has everything to do with your approach to this book. Tentatively, take the teachings as true and useful. But investigate them. As you read, test them out in your direct experience. The Buddha does not ask us to believe, but rather to understand and test his discoveries. Do the contemplations in this book help you get free, live wisely and with compassion?

I was raised in what you might call a tradition of skepticism. My father was the first to teach me the importance of asking questions. He came from a line of fourteen generations of rabbis, but, like his own ex-rabbi father, he rejected that heritage—although the term *rejected* is too weak. He frequently expressed contempt not only for Orthodox Judaism, but also for all religions. Before Hebrew school class, my father would pull me aside and say things such as, "Ask the rabbi just how Moses got that river to split." As you can imagine, Rabbi Minkowitz was not particularly pleased to be questioned in this way. I think my father was the first in recorded history to pay a rabbi *not* to give a talk at his son's bar mitzvah. My father said, "Please. Here's the money. *Don't* give a talk." But the rabbi did it. And my father fumed.

My father instilled in me his belief in the necessity of critical thinking. If I got into trouble—I was usually very good at home, but mischievous at school and in the neighborhood—my father put me on trial when he came home from work. He had always wanted to be a lawyer or judge, but he drove a cab, so he had to settle for a court made up of my mother and me. His court was sensitive and reasonable: he allowed "the accused" to speak, and sometimes, after listening, he dropped the charges. Of course, my mother would smile: they were both happy that I got off.

But my father always explained *why* I should have acted differently: "When you did that, your aunt Clara got aggravated, then she called up your mother, and now I have to listen to it. Next time, just pick up the rye bread and bagels and come home. It's simple." He made it clear that my actions had consequences. Above all, he taught me that everyone has the right to ask questions about anything and everything. With that right comes a responsibility: if you question the actions of others, you must also be willing to question your own.

Like my father, the Kalamas of the *Kalama Sutta* were skeptical but responsible. Their world was alive to spiritual matters, and overrun with teachers often competing for an audience and advocating different philosophies or paths. Their environment was not unlike the one you live in today. You're inundated with choices. "Interested in religion? What kind? Buddhism? What flavor? Vipassana? Oh, you've tried that? A little too dry, perhaps too much talk about suffering and impermanence? You might prefer Dzogchen, the innate perfection of the mind. Besides, most vipassana teachers are not even monks; they just wear sweatpants. At least the Tibetan teachers in their colorful outfits *look* like teachers. Or consider Zen. Beautiful! All those parables that teach you and make you laugh. Or what about the One Dharma approach that embraces them all?"

You live in a great swirling spiritual marketplace, full of promises and claims. No wonder many of you find it confusing. Twenty-five hundred years ago, the Kalamas were similarly confused by the profusion of paths to wisdom and peace. When the itinerant Buddha passed through their region, they gathered to hear his perspective:

> Lord, there are some brahmans and contemplatives who come to Kesaputta. They expound and glorify their own doctrines, but as for the doctrines of others, they deprecate them, revile them, show contempt for them, and disparage them. And then other brahmans and contemplatives come to Kesaputta. They expound and glorify their own doctrines, but as for the doctrines of others, they deprecate them, revile them, show contempt for them, and disparage them. They leave us absolutely uncertain and in doubt: Which of these venerable brahmans and contemplatives are speaking the truth, and which ones are lying?*

---

* From the *Kalama Sutta,* Anguttara Nikaya 3.65, translated from the Pali by Thanissaro Bhikkhu.

Though the Kalamas knew the Buddha's reputation as a great sage, they were concerned that he, too, might be merely one more teacher with a competing point of view. I deeply admire their uncommon degree of skepticism. The history of the world reveals that most of us are drawn to those who provide a strong, uncompromising teaching and who say or imply: "This is it, and everyone else is wrong." Certainly you see this dangerous pattern in contemporary politics. But it also shows up in spiritual circles, where it raises the same questions: Do you really want freedom? Can you handle the responsibility? Or would you just prefer an impressive teacher to provide answers and do the hard work for you?

Despite the host of problems in dharma centers in the past thirty years, I still see some yogis check their intelligence at the door, and almost grovel at the feet of a teacher, saying, "Just tell me how to live." Even with my staunch belief in questioning, I've made this mistake a few times myself. Have you? I longed for my special teacher with unique access to the truth. It felt fantastic to be their student. My spiritual life was taken care of. I was absolved of the worry and responsibility that comes with exercising the right to ask questions. But, of course, I wasn't free.

The Buddha's response to the concerns and confusions of the Kalamas gives you an antidote to making unskillful choices. He guides the Kalamas, and you, in the selection of a teacher and also in the skill of investigation in all realms of life:

> So, as I said, Kalamas: "Don't go by reports, by legends, by traditions, by scripture, by logical conjecture, by inference, by analogies, by agreement through pondering views, by probability, or by the thought, 'This contemplative is our teacher.' When you know for yourselves that, "These qualities are unskillful; these qualities are blameworthy; these qualities are criticized by the wise; these qualities, when adopted and carried out, lead to harm and to suffering"—then you should abandon them.' Thus was it said. And in reference to this was it said.

"Now, Kalamas, don't go by reports, by legends, by traditions, by scripture, by logical conjecture, by inference, by analogies, by agreement through pondering views, by probability, or by the thought, 'This contemplative is our teacher.' When you know for yourselves that, 'These qualities are skillful; these qualities are blameless; these qualities are praised by the wise; these qualities, when adopted and carried out, lead to welfare and to happiness'—then you should enter and remain in them."*

Before looking further into these teachings in this sutta, I'd like to offer another story. This one is said to have happened in a village in China where people came from far and wide to hear the dharma talks of a highly respected young teacher. One day, an esteemed old master joined the crowd. When the young teacher spotted him, he said, "Please, come up here, sit next to me while I give my talk." So the old master rose and sat at his side.

The young teacher resumed his talk and every other word out of his mouth quoted a sutta or a Zen master. The old teacher started to nod off in front of everyone. Though the young one noticed this out of the corner of his eye, he continued. The more authorities he cited, the sleepier the old master appeared. Finally, the young teacher interrupted himself to ask, "What's wrong? Is my teaching so boring, so awful, so totally off?" At that point, the old master leaned over and gave him a hard pinch. The young teacher screamed, "Ouch!" The old master said, "Ah! That's what I've traveled this long distance to hear. This pure teaching. This 'ouch' teaching."

Like the old master in this Zen story, the Buddha's response to the Kalamas highlights the primacy of direct experience. The Buddha acknowledges that people rely on multiple types of authority: some internal, some external, some reliable, some way off the mark. He

---

* From the *Kalama Sutta*, Anguttara Nikaya 3.65, translated from the Pali by Thanissaro Bhikkhu, *Access to Insight*, www.accesstoinsight.org/tipitaka/an/ano3/ano3.065.than.html, retrieved on May 1, 2013.

advises them that just because a teaching is ancient, or recited from the scripture, does not make it true. Just because it appears reasonable, or you're drawn to the person teaching it, does not mean it is wise.

Then the question becomes: How do you distinguish authentic from false or misguided? Where do you turn for guidance to learn how to live?

In the *Kalama Sutta*, the Buddha does not reject reason and logic. He does not say that ancient teachings are irrelevant, or that you have to reinvent the dharma wheel every time you face a choice. After all, at this moment, by writing this book, I put these teachings into action, based on a body of dharma teachings that stretch across generations of dharma ancestors. If you and I do not study the texts and listen to the teachings, how will we find what has been criticized and praised by the wise? No, the Buddha gives the Kalamas—and us—guidelines that are *precautions, not prohibitions.* He cautions us against blind obedience to the authority of traditions and teachers, or to the authority of our own ideas. He also cautions against blind obedience to reason and logic.

For students new to meditative living, these warnings can be especially relevant. On first coming to practice, you will find that convictions inspired by teachings, teachers, and community support help motivate and energize you to begin to practice. However, this faith is provisional. Remember, the Buddha tells you to test the teachings and ideas as "working hypotheses" in the laboratory of your actions. There is an "expiration date" when conviction based on external support gives way to conviction grounded in personal experience.

At that point, your understanding is no longer borrowed from others. It is authentic and your own. This happens as you develop the ability to awaken and stabilize mindfulness.

Whether you are a new or experienced meditator, when you truly investigate your beliefs and convictions, don't you find that it challenges and stretches you? This has certainly been my experience. Teachings can inspire you. Just to hear them can satisfy your intellect and nourish your emotions. Even so, as you read or practice the three steps in this book, remember to ask: Where is this taking me?

Does the practice of breath awareness or choiceless awareness move me in a direction to act with more kindness and wisdom? Investigate again and again.

But don't stop there. For the Dharma to become firsthand knowledge—to feel the "ouch" of it—you have to live intimately with it, hold it up to scrutiny, and let it hold you up to scrutiny. "Be a lamp unto yourself," says the Buddha. Your questions light the way. This is the heart of the *Kalama Sutta*.

Ultimately, your ideas of the truth must be put to the test of lived experience. Throughout his teachings, the Buddha offers a simple formula that guides us in this direction: examine everything in terms of cause and effect. Whatever is unskillful, leading to harm or suffering for you and others, should be recognized and abandoned. Whatever is skillful, leading to happiness and peace for you and others, should be pursued.

Remember, early in his life as a teacher, the Buddha said, "I teach one thing only: suffering and the end of suffering." And he gave us a set of practices that emphasize learning how to live and how to lessen suffering, called the four noble truths: there is suffering; there is a cause of suffering, which is craving and attachment; there is cessation of suffering; and there is a path of practice that brings about this cessation.

The four noble truths are my unfailing compass for every form of life, whether teaching in a meditation hall or encountering a stranger on the street. For thousands of years, they have been shared by every school of Buddhism and guided countless yogis. As you practice the three steps to awareness, the four noble truths offer the vehicle to learn the skills to diminish suffering in the world, even to free yourself from suffering. The first noble truth, *there is suffering*, describes an unskillful outcome: the emergence and recognition of suffering. The second noble truth, *craving and attachment*, is the unskillful cause that brings about this harmful outcome. The third noble truth, *cessation of suffering*, is a skillful outcome brought about by following the fourth noble truth, *an eightfold path* characterized by ethics, stability of mind, and wisdom.

Yet even the most fundamental teachings of the Buddha, such as the four noble truths, deserve to be held up to the light of inquiry described in the *Kalama Sutta*. I learned this in my early days as a vipassana yogi, when the Thai forest master Ajahn Chah visited the Insight Meditation Society in Barre, Massachusetts. At that time, many of us were enthralled with the liberating power of "letting go." In our discussions, everyone was letting go of this and letting go of that—and often letting go of "merely everything." As he listened, Ajahn Chah seemed to grow skeptical. He encouraged us to slow down, back up, and carefully examine the moments when we were actually suffering. Rather than rush to let go, he urged us to make direct contact with the suffering and to see whether it was caused by some form of craving and attachment, of wanting things to be other than the way they were. He felt that the *real* letting go was learned by seeing the price we paid by holding on and resisting—and the joy experienced when we were free of the burden of attachment.

Paying attention to our own experience of suffering, rather than our conceptual notions of letting go, gave us the chance to see the benefits of the four noble truths in the crucible of our own lives. This form of seeing and learning, so emphatically expressed in the *Kalama Sutta*, is at the core of the teachings that follow on the pages of this book. The transformation of suffering that comes from awareness is most powerful when it's intimate with the experience of your own life. Inquire, question, and test your understanding of the teachings so that it becomes bone deep.

PART ONE

Practicing Awareness

1

Whole-Body
Breath Awareness

· · · · · · ·

One trains oneself; sensitive to the whole body, I breath in.
Sensitive to the whole body, I breath out.
—THE BUDDHA, *Anapanasati Sutta*

THE BREATH IS A VEHICLE designed to help us learn the lessons that
life has to teach us. It is there in the service of awareness. It is there
as a kind of friend or companion to accompany us, to support us,
to help us develop a mind that's clear, stable, relaxed, and energetic.
The *Anapanasati Sutta* uses conscious breathing to develop the mind
so it's a fit instrument to see into itself. Breathing is used to awaken
and then to maintain full attention to the process of mind and body,
on and off the cushion. A mind that's developed in this way can then
look at the things that are difficult and known to all of us. It can look
at fear, loneliness, anger. It can help you to get to know yourself, to
understand how you *actually* live—and through this understanding,
free you.

The particular approach to the *Anapanasati Sutta* that we will
be using is very simple. As stated earlier, it is called the condensed
method. Basically, there are two steps. In one step, called *shamatha*,
you calm the mind with conscious breathing. In the second, you use

that mind, which is now more steady, clear, and supported by sensitivity to breathing, to watch everything arise and pass away. This is vipassana, or insight meditation. It includes all the events that we call the mind: emotions, thoughts, plans, worries, the conditions of the body, sounds, smells—everything we think of as our experience. Breathing awareness is not just about calming the mind—a common assumption among meditators not familiar with this method. Rather, the breath helps you maintain full attention, enabling you to see with greater clarity and accuracy the true nature of all forms: everything that arises passes away. The implications of such insightful seeing can be profound and liberating.

Right now, let's turn attention to the first part of the practice, which calms the mind and familiarizes you with the breath as it is experienced throughout the whole body. In the next chapter, you'll start seeing how the letting go happens, as you learn how to use the breath as a home base while watching whatever arises and passes away. Further on, we'll investigate how the breath helps you to develop greater sensitivity to how you actually live your lives, as you go through your daily experiences off the cushion, whether at work, in school, or at home. Then we'll move into the practice of sitting with no agenda at all, actually moving beyond the breath and into the awareness of silence.

Let's begin the full-fledged practice of breath awareness as you will work with it in your formal meditation. We'll start with a translation of the third of the sixteen steps in the sutta itself: "Being sensitive to the whole body, the yogi breathes in. Being sensitive to the whole body, the yogi breathes out." The frame of reference is the whole body, sitting. This implies that you experience each breath as it turns up in you, however that is. It's not a desperate search. It's not trying to encompass the entire body. It's just feeling whatever you feel. That's good enough.

What's crucial is the quality of awareness. The sensations turn up more distinctively in different places in the body from breath to breath, and this helps train the mind because it's challenging. Not only is the mind learning to be attentive, but also to be supple, flexible. It is learning to stay with breath sensations as they emerge, whatever their quality, wherever they are most vivid.

SITTING MEDITATION

Wisdom has everything to do with learning how to live. And this learning requires not just a mind that's interested and fit to learn, but also the help of the body. They're close partners.

In the sitting practice but also beyond sitting, can you help the body to relax and to be upright as well?

Both are necessary. Relaxation alone can become a kind of casual attitude that makes it difficult to be alert. Uprightness alone can become rigid, compromising your ability to relax the body. Here, you're learning how to fine-tune your attention just as you would fine-tune the volume on a radio. One way it's a little too loud, the other a little too low. Finally, if you're listening to music that you love and really want to hear, you find the right way to calibrate it so that the volume is just perfect. This is an ongoing project of helping the body learn how to sit. In dharma circles it's called *acquiring a seat.* Just plopping yourself down on the cushion to sit is not enough.

The standard used to guide you is the same as with any other yogic posture, or *asana,* as it was originally applied and as it remains today. As you become established in a particular position, the body learns to be both steady and comfortable, and it's helpful if both qualities are present. As the body learns how to be stable and relaxed, you are provided with a strong foundation from which to pay attention.

Of course, this is an ideal. At the outset of practice, you are usually neither! What to do? You start by arranging the body to be as upright and comfortable as you are able to manage, and gradually learn your way into a more satisfactory way of sitting. It's a good idea to take a few moments at the start of a sitting and course through the body with mindfulness to see any obvious places of tension. Begin with the head and slowly move down through the entire body, pausing when attention is called for. Perhaps the jaw is squeezed shut with determination. Don't try to relax this area. Simply visit the discomfort with sensitivity and feel what you label as "tension" in a raw, naked way. See what happens and move on. Are the shoulders hunched up in eager anticipation? What is this like? Stay a few moments; see what happens and move on until the entire body is observed.

You are not striving to attain a perfectly upright, relaxed body; you are trying to make a brief survey of its condition to help settle down and enter into the practice of whole-body breath awareness.

By the way, if at any point during one of your sitting periods you conclude that you need to shift your posture because of sleepiness or extreme discomfort or pain in the body, do so—but try to keep movement of the body to a minimum. Pause, reflect. Why is it necessary to shift position? Don't do it immediately. For whatever reason, if you decide to move, do it slowly, mindfully. Breathe in and breathe out, so there's breath awareness accompanying the shift. It's also fine to stand, doing the very same practice in the standing position.

If you find that you tend to immediately change your posture because of every little itch or condition of discomfort, try to sit with that and see how annoyed you get and how desperate the mind becomes. "Oh, if I could only scratch that, I would be the happiest person on the planet." If the mind gets that desperate about an itch, think of what it can do about all the other things that come up in life. Sometimes it's good to sit and be aware of how the mind works. At other times, you may be doing yourself harm and taking all the joy out of practice if you refuse to budge, despite extreme discomfort. There's no pat answer. That's wisdom's job: knowing when it's wise to move and when it isn't.

Let's begin this practice of whole-body breath awareness. When you're sitting on your cushion, chair, or bench, bring attention to the obvious fact that you're sitting. Sitting is happening. You put your full attention on the body sitting the way it is. No strain is involved.

Don't struggle to try to encompass every inch of the body. Just inhabit the whole body in a relaxed and easy way, feeling the breath sensations wherever you feel them. As an in-breath happens, where do you feel it? And as the lungs empty, where do you feel the breath sensations? Wherever you feel it is fine.

This practice is about developing whole-body breath awareness. What is your attitude toward the process of breathing? You may discover a strong tendency to control the breath—to direct, hold back, or lengthen the breath. In the same way, most of us attempt to direct other aspects of life, using A as a stepping-stone to get to B or, if you're very ambitious, skipping ahead to Z. If so, is this old habit-energy asserting itself? Are you striving to make the breath more vivid so you can "get calm" more quickly?

Now you are being asked to leave things alone, to not intervene, to simply sit and watch. Passive, fatalistic? Can anything worthwhile come about this way? Please give these instructions a try and find out. Perhaps you observe that you are, in fact, controlling the breath. If you try to not control the breath, you're caught in a subtler trap of controlling the controlling, which is futile. Instead, bring mindfulness to this tendency: become aware of "controllingness." You are learning the art of *allowing*, of letting the breathing happen, not making it happen. Whatever rhythm it assumes is just fine.

In recent weeks, I've observed my granddaughter as she learns how to walk. I watch her fall down, get up, fall down again, then get up again. This goes on for quite a while. What's striking to me is her absence of comparison to other children. Clearly, she is not thinking, "Hey, the child next door does not fall down as often as I do," or "By this age, the doctors say I should fall down after four steps and I only reached three and a half." No. I see her joyfully participate in the process of learning how to walk: no suffering. But the parents and grandparents present a different picture. Because they are burdened by the latest medical norms that standardize and dictate "correct" progress in walking, they compare their child to others, which leads to suffering. Like all of us, they would suffer less if they more fully developed the art of allowing.

As you practice mindful breathing, you develop this art, and you also cultivate the related ability to *receive*. You are simply present to breath sensations as they emerge, wherever they are present in the body. Not groping or searching, you are just being sensitive to what enters your field of awareness. The two go together: allowing and, at the same time, receiving the experience of whole-body breathing.

Can you learn to develop the capacity to be steady and mindful, whether or not the breath is pleasant, vivid, or distinctive? As your practice unfolds, can you maintain this attitude in the face of the full range of mental, emotional, and physical events, which at times will be far more daunting?

Perhaps as you open to the body breathing, you feel that the jaw, as part of bodily life, is very tense. It is not that you decide to focus on the energy in that part of the body. Rather, it asserts itself into your awareness, in the same time frame as breath sensations. Start noticing the breathing throughout the body. As your attention is drawn to the jaw, you also feel breath sensations within the context of the body sitting. Breath, mindfulness, and body are synchronized as a unitary experience. These are actual sensations. You can feel them as the lungs fill up and empty. For those of you who are new to this practice, please know that this is not referring to an image or picture or word. Images and thoughts are made in the mind. Right now, you are immersing your attention in raw, naked, bodily life. See what happens in the light of full attention.

In this practice of whole-body breath awareness, you're allowing the breath to happen naturally. There's no way in which you're attempting to fashion the breath. You're not trying to shape it into some ideal way of breathing. It's not a form of breath therapy, although some of you who have done it for a while know that it does have a very beneficial effect on breathing. You're learning a new art: the art of allowing and receiving. Can you let the breath happen rather than make it happen? You're not running after anything. You're upright and relaxed, an invitation for awareness, breathing, and body to come together. Little by little, it becomes a unitary experience. The three energies merge into each other: body, mind, and breath. Of course they were never separate!

If you have experience in yoga, you might have developed the habit of controlling and directing the breath in the practice of prana-yama. That's a valuable skill, but you're not doing that right now. If you're an experienced meditator and have practiced other meth-ods of breath awareness, a different kind of difficulty may emerge. Most methods of breath awareness are focused and one-pointed, either on the nostrils, chest, or abdomen. In this practice, in con-trast to narrowing down, you're encouraged to open and expand the field of awareness with attention, shifting as breath energy draws you to different parts of the body, from one in- and out-breath to another. This can feel awkward. You might feel incompetent, like a complete beginner, as habit-energy from the past insists on being focused on where it had been comfortable and effective. A strug-gle ensues. You're not sure you even want to learn this whole-body breath awareness stuff.

Of course, you have the freedom to stay with what has been helpful in the past. But if you decide to give this new way a try, re-member that you've been through this awkwardness before with any new learning project. Watch the mind struggling. Wherever there is resistance, there's also a beautiful opportunity for wisdom to de-velop, by seeing what is happening: "I don't like this." "It's new to me, it doesn't feel good." "What if I fail at it?" You see the mind struggle.

Patience, gentle persistence, and a certain amount of real interest are needed to learn any new skill. If you fall asleep again, you wake up again, without blame, just like my granddaughter falling down and often even gleefully getting up as she learns to walk. Wouldn't it be wonderful if you could be so simple? Just learning a new skill. No keeping score. No comparing. This has happened to you before and it may happen again. You're going to wake up, fall asleep, wake up, fall asleep. Those who most benefit from the practice don't get discouraged, or if they do, they mindfully pick themselves up and begin again.

As you all know, the mind is wild—especially at the beginning. It has a mind of its own. It hears the instructions and doesn't care.

It has other preoccupations far more interesting than the breath, such as worrying about what's going to happen twenty years from now, when Social Security benefits run out, or reliving something that happened twenty years ago, when you ran in a marathon. Even though right now you are "officially" emphasizing concentration and calming practice, one of the things you begin to see is that your mind very often prefers an imaginary future, either wonderful or horrible, or a past that's over with, never to return, that was wonderful or horrible: anything but the fact of a simple in- or out-breath. You begin to see certain compulsions of mind and how the mind prefers a conceptual reality to the simple, naked truth of here and now.

Right at that moment, practice is so exquisitely simple. You come back to each breath just as it happens and just as it's experienced throughout the body. You come back as many times as you need to: gently, gracefully, with ease. No need to turn it into a problem. If the mind starts keeping score—thinking, evaluating, comparing itself with how it thinks other people might be doing or how it did yesterday—then see that. Those are just thoughts. If you believe in them, you have a problem. You can learn to just let them come and go, and once again take up whole-body breath awareness.

As the breath smoothes out, becoming more subtle and fine, you may find a large gap of silence between breaths. It is easy to get lost there, filling up the stillness by spinning out, imagining, projecting, inventing a future or reliving the past. Minutes can go by until you realize you're lost in mind stuff. One advantage of the whole-body approach is that although there's a gap between breaths, the body is still there, sitting. You're aware of this "sittingness" until the next breath emerges. It gives the mind something tangible to hold onto to help it stay awake in the present moment.

Using whole-body awareness, you're learning to become intimate with the raw, naked experience of bodily life. As you do this, you're emphasizing the first foundation of mindfulness, "the body in the body." It's not so easy to do, because it's always mixed in with the mind. But as you sit and breathe, just bring attention to the whole body. You can learn not to try to fix anything, not to intervene, not to use things to get somewhere. You just allow breath energy to emerge, disclose itself, and depart.

Breathing in, where do you feel the breath sensation? Breathing out, where do you feel it? You maintain this sense of bodily sensations that come and go. It's not imagination. It's not an image. You're just learning this art of allowing, which in more religious language would be called *surrender*. Surrender to what? To *what is,* to the natural law that the breath is obeying as the lungs fill up and empty.

As you follow this way of practice, you take your seat and you're upright and relaxed. You're sitting, breathing, and learning how to stay with one theme: breathing in the context of the whole body. As you do that, of course, the world doesn't stop. Wherever you are, there are sounds. Some of them are pleasant, like the birds singing "chirp, chirp." Others are not so pleasant, such as the trucks, cars, ambulances, and police cars that speed up and down city streets. Letting sounds come and go, you're learning to peacefully coexist with all that's other than breath.

Thoughts also come and go. So do moods and images. Likewise, the body feels comfortable, then uncomfortable. The mind is optimistic, then pessimistic. You are totally interested in practice, then bored with it. Throughout it all, make your home in whole-body breath awareness. The breath is like a good friend helping to support that awareness. Every time you're with an in-breath or out-breath, you're learning how to be in the present moment. You're learning how to be with the breath sensations just as they are. It's actually an advantage that the breath takes on so many different qualities, for this challenges the mind to learn how to stay awake with the breath when it's long, when it's shallow, when it's fine, when it's coarse.

This comprehensive approach can be especially helpful for intellectual people, because there's no verbal content; the intellect isn't being fed. In this approach, you're not for or against thought. You're not trying to fix anything, not trying to use the breath as a stepping-stone to get anywhere. Rather, you allow the mind to think itself in whatever way it wishes. You're learning how to temporarily let things happen. You're learning how to let the mind do what it does without grasping on to futuristic imaginings or remembrances of days gone by. Each breath only happens in the present moment—and you're learning how to dwell in that moment, using the breath to help you awaken and maintain full attention.

One meaning of mindfulness is to remember to turn toward what it is you've decided to turn toward. In this case, it's keeping in mind whole-body breathing. Out of all the many interesting places for your attention to land, you've taken this: the body, sitting and breathing. Whether a production of the mind is profound or trivial, it's a distraction. The point is to come back to the utter simplicity of sitting and breathing and knowing. That's why it's important for you to know what you've set out to do. At least for now, commit yourself to this method. If you're vague about it, the door is opened for the wild untrained mind to reinstate itself and take over.

As you become aware of the breathing, it does become calmer. Now as it becomes calmer, you may find, as I think millions have found for thousands of years, that the body becomes more relaxed, because the breath is a powerful conditioner of the body. You may also find that the mind becomes calmer, because the breath is a powerful conditioner of the mind. You're not trying to calm it—it just happens as a by-product of mindfulness. And of course it goes in the other direction. Relaxing the body relaxes the mind, and relaxing the mind helps the breath. What you also may see is that as this is sustained, the body follows suit and it becomes easier to sit. Maybe not all at once, but little by little, as breath awareness becomes more continuous, something very good comes out of it—you feel more calm, more peaceful. There's joy. Otherwise, why bother doing it? If you haven't experienced it, you will. It's not mysterious. As the breath awareness develops, the body starts to relax because they're all interrelated. Finally, you'll see that it is just one life happening.

Remember, though, you're not trying to calm anything. The instructions are to allow the breath to just happen in the context of the whole body—period, full stop. When you practice in order to get somewhere, you're not fully observant or mindful. For example, if the mind says, "Wow, if you really stay with the breath, you get really really calm and you get joyful and peaceful. I want a piece of that." OK, the truth is that does happen. But if it's on your mind as you're watching the breath, then a corner of your mind is distracted and goal-oriented: "I will do this in order to get that." But this is an art, the art of allowing. The calm that you want will come out of the seeing. If you're trying to use the seeing to get the calm, then it's a struggle and you begin to experience suffering.

It's not a matter of searching for breath sensations. It's more the art of receiving whatever is there. It's learning the art of allowing, seeing if you can let the breath breathe itself and receiving it as it happens. No matter what the quality of the breathing, the challenge is to stay awake with that particular quality. You're not trying to shape the breath or fashion it in any way whatsoever. You're not trying to approximate it to some norm of what we think of as healthy breathing. Rather, you're learning to just simply allow breath to happen. When you don't, you see that. And in the seeing, little by little, you naturally come to that place of noninterference. It's by seeing interference, seeing how you direct the breath—and this can be extremely subtle—that the power of such controlling starts to seep out of the mind and you learn the art of just being present.

Any time you're taken away from the body breathing, can you see it without turning it into a problem, fault, or mistake? Distractions from breath sensations are not a setback unless you get caught up in them. As soon as you wake up, as soon as you become aware of unawareness, you're back on track. Just ease back to the breath once again, to the sitting body breathing, whole-body breathing. As many times as you drift off, that many times, come back. Come back gently, gracefully, without blame. Often the mind will activate certain habit-energies, evaluate how you're doing, and give you a report card with a low grade. Just see the mind doing that. It can't help itself. Thoughts come and go, like clouds. Then return to the breathing. Two thousand times in one sitting, or just once.

Remember, at the beginning, everyone's mind is untamed. In all my years of teaching, I haven't known one exception, no matter what a person's occupation or level of concentration, whether in music, computer programming, cooking, or parenting. It doesn't matter. When it comes to looking at ourselves, it seems to be a new and challenging beginning.

Step number one is seeing that this is our condition. The actual state of the mind is wild. It has to be trained. It has to be reeducated. You haven't learned the value of not running after every production of thought. You haven't learned how much energy is squandered believing every thought, how you are taken on a trip by chronic introspection and repetitive thoughts. When you look at them carefully, you see they have very little significance. Just habit-energy, like a broken machine repeating itself again and again and again.

Some years ago, a world-famous brain surgeon came to our center in Cambridge to learn how to meditate. After about a month of teaching sessions and personal interviews, he asked to speak to me privately. He informed me that he did not wish to continue practicing. I probed for the reason why, and he reported, sadly, that the discovery of how chaotic his mind was—compared with the exquisite, stable level of attention that he was used to while operating on people's brains—left him feeling humiliated. His honesty was impressive, but despite my encouragement, he never returned. Apparently, he could look into other people's brains, but not his own!

So please do not get discouraged; it's a brand-new skill you are learning. Keep at it! Once you start to see that the mind has to be trained, and you simply rest in the breathing, the tendency to be pulled away from the breathing starts to weaken. You start to see the benefits of conscious breathing because it brings real peace and joy and perhaps other benefits that you can't put into words. As this happens, you start to unlearn old and unexamined ways in which the mind has behaved, dwelling in a past that's never to return or constantly conjuring up the future. Can you trade that in for just this ordinary in-breath, just this ordinary out-breath?

The practice is just being where you are. It's not easy. All of us seem to prefer that imaginary future or a past that's over with—

anything but right now. Why that's so varies with each person. But often it's because you have an idea about yourself. You think, "This is me breathing and I want to excel." You want to be a great yogi. You want to be calm. You want to do it right. And no doubt, that dynamic is not new. You didn't get infected with it when you started to practice. Most likely, you've already done this regarding money or sex or art or fame or beauty or clothing. You have endless ways of making yourself suffer. Comparing is suffering. You may have an imaginary schema of where you're supposed to be in this practice. But the instructions are simple: Be where you are.

If you can see the suffering that comes from ideas about yourself, that's wisdom. You realize you made up a goal about where you think you're supposed to be, and that you fell short. But it's all made up in the mind. You are simply being encouraged to wake up to the fact that the body is sitting and breathing. That's all. But many of us are far too educated and complicated for such simplicity.

Let's elaborate on what has already been said, putting it in context, adding a bit more detail. Begin by arranging the body in a posture that is as comfortable and upright as you can manage. Course through the body, starting from the head and moving down to your feet. Feel any tension, tightness, or other forms of discomfort. Briefly visit that discomfort with mindfulness, and move on. No need to seek perfection. Now inhabit the entire body with awareness, your actual physical form sitting and expressing itself through sensations and movements of energy. If for any reason you have been cut off from bodily life, this may at first feel quite alien. With some practice, you develop a more intimate and satisfying ability to rest in the sitting body just as it is.

The next step is crucial: you give relaxed, careful attention to respiration and to the obvious, often neglected fact that each one of us is breathing. In other words, you are alive! Did you know that? You're not trying to make anything be other than what it is, nor get anywhere. Simply being sensitive to this in-breath as you feel it in the whole body. This out-breath, the same. Gentle, relaxed, and alert. Just as a mirror reflects what's in front of it, your awareness becomes simple and nonreactive, just reflecting what's there.

Sounds great, doesn't it? You hear someone like me say, "Just allow the breath to flow naturally." But most of you use more control of the breath than you realize. You can't help it. At times, you may find that the tendency to control the breath—lengthening or shortening the breath sensations' duration—makes the inhalations and exhalations more pleasant and appealing. When it's more pleasant, it's easier to maintain mindfulness; when it's more unpleasant, it's more difficult.

So what to do? As I mentioned earlier, if you try to not control the breath, that's more control: an exhausting struggle. Instead, just experience the controllingness of the mind; learn to maintain steady attention, independent of the quality of each breath sensation. Don't get into a war with it. Don't try to smooth anything out. You're learning a vital skill, which is to just be with whatever comes up—because it's there.

You are not feeling the word *breath*. You're feeling the actual contact and the reverberations can be felt throughout the body. When you get really quiet you can feel breath sensations in your toes or your forehead or your back. Don't try to force that; if it happens, fine. If not, that's fine, too. Feel the breath wherever you feel it. Some feel it more in the nostril, others in the abdomen, because that's been your practice in the past. That's where you feel it. Don't decide a priori that you're going to focus your attention in those places. You're there because it's more vivid and has caught your attention, just as it might be more vivid elsewhere in the body for someone else, or for you in another moment of your sitting.

Every moment of mindfulness reeducates the mind and helps develop a new skill of steadiness, sensitivity, and watching. You become more alert to what's happening, how life is behaving, and especially how your life is behaving right here and right now. As you practice whole-body breath awareness, you become more present to your experience and less caught up in proliferations of the mind, or what is called, in Pali, *papancas:* states that arise when one thought begets an emotion, which begets another thought about the emotion. Before you know it, you're living in an alternative reality of cascading thoughts and emotions that have nothing to do with what's going on.

More and more, too, you come to know the body from inside. This knowledge is not like studying anatomy or physiology. Instead, you get to know the body as a field of energy. You become more sensitive to it. There's a chiropractor who I've seen for years, and I've sent a lot of people to him. He told me, "I am always happy when your people show up." I said, "Why is that? He said, "Well, when I ask them a question about how their body feels, they can answer with precision, because they're in touch with their bodies."

This is part of that reeducation. It may not be liberation, but it will help you become more intimate with your body. Often the nervous system starts to improve. Your energy increases. You become more sensitive to food and its impact on you, to climate and its impact on you, or to the affects of taking particular medications. There are also many health benefits. The nervous system, including the brain, is soothed. You enjoy a respite from your preoccupations. There is an enormous intelligence in the body that's been stunted because you've misused or neglected it. Many wonderful body practices such as hatha yoga and tai chi are now available and can help awaken this intelligence—and so can the approach of breath awareness.

Some of you may find that you have difficulty with the breathing. If that happens, there are a number of ways to resolve that problem. You might drop the breath for the moment and just pay attention to simple body sensations. Pause, reflect. Are you trying too hard? Do you have some unacknowledged idea of how practice should be by now? If so, where does this goal come from? In the end, the practice is all about attention. The breath is designed to help you pay attention because it cuts down on unnecessary thinking. If you become fixated on anything, even a good thing, it will backfire on you. You might vow, "I will pay attention to the breath and set the world's

Olympic record for uninterrupted breath awareness." But gold medals have nothing to do with wisdom or becoming more free.

Waking up is becoming more alive. The aliveness that's available to all of you is already here in this moment. It's life in the form of breathing. You're learning how to peacefully coexist with sounds, thoughts, smells, images, moods, and productions of the mind. But your primary object of attention, your meditation theme for the moment, is just this simple fact of sitting and breathing and knowing it.

You could say your life unfolds on two tracks. There's the track of the mind, where you are being governed by giving over authority to the productions of the mind. On this track, you're almost exclusively thinking your way through life. The mind is between you and the raw, naked, intimate experience of life itself.

The other track is the dharma track. You're awake. You're in a state of attention. You're present. You're directly in touch with your experience, unmediated by ideas, images, conclusions, or notions. Just this! At this very moment, whether you know it or not, each breath happens right here and right now. Little by little the question becomes, Are you intimate with this breath just as it is? Intimate, meaning not separate but fully experiencing whatever you experience as the breath fills up the lungs and empties in this particular posture at this time in this place.

When the mind gets caught up in its productions, can you return to the body and the breathing? Wherever you feel those breath sensations at any moment, your practice is perfect. This new skill refines your ability to live in the state of observation, of awareness. When you go off the dharma track (notice I said *when*, not *if*), you come back, not judging or being harsh with yourself, and not getting discouraged. Patience allows you to skip all that evaluating and criticizing. The practice is the coming back. In fact, when aware that you are *not* aware, you have already come back. If you didn't need to come back, because the mind is so untrained and wild, you wouldn't need to practice. So please don't turn sitting and breathing into a problem. The great Thai forest master Ajahn Chah calls meditation "a holiday for the heart."

A lot of what you're learning is a form of reeducation, so that the mind learns new ways of relating to itself. You're not constantly turning authority over to the realm of thought, to the past or future, to knowledge and past experience, to conditioning. Sometimes it's appropriate to use your accumulations from the past. But life is often better without it. When you are aware of your breath, more and more the mind becomes freer. It sees accurately. And this seeing is the beginning of wisdom. It helps you understand how you actually live, and in the process, to live more intelligently,

In the following pages, you'll bring whole-body breath awareness into the four postures, including the practice of walking meditation. From there, you'll go beyond the breath and body to include every aspect of what we call being alive as a human being. Whether walking or sitting, whole-body breath awareness helps you establish a home base, a point of stability from which you can learn to widen your capacity to receive and observe every expression of your own experience, intimately and without reactivity. This will bring you to the second step of the condensed method: from shamatha, or concentrated calm, to vipassana, insight meditation. Can you learn to look and listen, and to learn from what you see and hear?

· · · · ·

Q: *I can't figure out the best breath awareness technique. Some of my teachers suggest that we choose one place, yet you encourage us to be mindful of breath sensations in the whole body. I'm confused.*

A: Yes, working with different teachers can easily generate confusion. We dharma teachers can get attached to our particular method and deliver the teachings forcefully. In my early days of practice, various teachers of breath awareness featured the nostrils, upper lip below the nostril, abdomen, chest, and whole body. Most encouraged us to allow the breath to assume its own pace; some to gently control the breathing to make the process more comfortable. Most included the in- and out-breath; some emphasized just the out-breath. All made a convincing case for their preference.

What to do? I gave each approach my best effort while working with a given teacher and my conclusion was—they were all correct! Each method proved to be valuable.

While you practice a particular method, it can be helpful to believe that your technique—or your teacher or lineage or meditation center—is the best. You feel fortunate. This mobilizes energy and often inspires strong practice. But as you grow on the path, more ingenuity is called for. You have to become self-reliant and see what you need from moment to moment. Just watch out for compulsive shopping around, which stems from the restless mind and its refusal to sustain any effort.

If the teachings and the teacher come together, you're fortunate indeed. Remember, too, that no matter where the breath is most vivid right now—the tummy, nose, or chest—it will change because the law of impermanence is at work here, too. If you choose one location rather than whole-body breathing, fine. Keep going.

For me, approaches to mindfulness and concentration need to be adjusted to our unique character structure and temperament. The same holds true for all your meditation practices: choose the method that helps you let go of grasping and attachment. If it does, it is in the service of the Dharma. You may learn the approach from a little-known teacher who never wrote a book or presented at a Buddhist conference. Find out what is skillful for you, and don't worry about what is useful for the person sitting next to you. This investigation requires patience and honesty. As you do it, it's a practice—not a waste of time.

. . . . .

Q: I became so focused on the sensations in various parts of my body that I wasn't sure whether or not I was breathing. It was very disorienting.

A: I understand. Obviously, the mind is involved in whatever you do. The breath is just the breath, and then the human mind makes up what it thinks is happening. It makes up a story, it interprets, and it manufactures "disorienting." The key question is, Have you lost touch with sitting and breathing? Because if you move away, even to a highly interesting place, it is a distraction. You're no longer doing this particular practice that emphasizes the whole-body breathing.

· · · · ·

Q: *I have fairly solid ideas of what breathing is, and how the air molecules move through the diaphragm . . .*

A: Perhaps you are a scientist. Someone else is an artist, and they see paint strokes in the mind. A flower-lover experiences the fragrance of the breath. These are all interesting. I'm not banishing them. But each mind will construct and interpret the world. When these productions of the mind crop up, your instructions are to say, "Thank you very much," and then return to the breath. Whether profound or trivial, they are a distraction. Don't fight with them or get lost in them. Come back to the utter simplicity of sitting and breathing and knowing. Be aware of the raw sensations that occur as the lungs empty and fill up again. The rest is extra.

· · · · ·

Q: *Often I notice enormous disappointment in myself for not coming back to the breath—especially after I hear instructions to do this. Am I working too hard? Should I try to examine the contents of my mind?*

A: Most people are familiar with disappointment after hearing instructions to follow the breath. One approach would be to see that you may have an ambition in the mind: Are you trying to get somewhere? Perhaps you want to become extremely calm or highly concentrated on the breath. Once you create this condition, you lay the groundwork for what the Buddha termed *dukkha,* or suffering. You measure yourself against a goal, and because you have not achieved it, you judge yourself. This produces the mental toxin of ill will toward yourself or someone else. All of us can turn ourselves into battlefields.

No doubt, this dynamic did not begin when you sat on your

cushion. Right now, it's the breath, but it could be anything: sex, beauty, fame, iPads. When you compare, you suffer.

Put another way, don't be disappointed about feeling disappointed. Just see it! Awareness is never disappointed—it simply sees. If you are observing, you are not identified; if you are identified, you are not observing. What happens to disappointment in the light of awareness?

If you do investigate the mind at work, then you are practicing vipassana. For some people, this is a better place to start than with samadhi. This may be true for you. Perhaps you become calm by watching many objects come and go, rather than focusing on only one. At a certain point, you might feel calm enough to do classical samadhi with the breath again.

Whatever approach you use, as you see the suffering that comes from comparisons, you have the chance to develop wisdom. You realize that your mind manufactured a goal and then fell short of it. The instructions are to simply breath and know it. That's it. Sounds simple, but at first, it may not be easy.

·   ·   ·   ·   ·

Q: I've noticed that even when I meditate, my breath doesn't seem to move naturally. I control it. Then I try not to control it, which brings anxiety into my body. Sometimes it seems way too stressful to try to stay calm.

A: You hear someone like me say, "Just allow the breath to flow naturally," and it sounds wonderful. Then suddenly "you" come into the picture. This happens to most of us. The ego swoops in and creates a melodrama. It decides that there is "cash value" in the natural breath. It wants credit for this. "If it weren't for me," it says, "you wouldn't be breathing. We will get enlightened together."

What to do? If you try to not control the breath, that's more control. You struggle and it's tiring. But remember, this approach is utterly simple. As you've heard me say many times by now—but it bears repeating—you just experience the controllingness of the mind. You don't get into a war with it or try to smooth it out. As you see the mind try to extend or restrain the breathing, the very seeing calms the breath.

But let's say you miss that moment of mindfulness and suddenly you become anxious, or my words make you anxious. We will look at this closely in the next section of these teachings, when we practice with the breath and all expressions of the mind-body process. Right now, remember that as you become aware of the breath, it grows calm. That just happens—as long as you don't throw in extra material. Little by little, as breath awareness develops, the body relaxes. The calmness is a byproduct of the awareness of breathing.

* * * * *

Q: *Whenever my mind becomes calm and slows down, I often start to drift off to sleep. When that happens, I pull myself back to awareness of the breath. Is that part of a good practice?*

A: Yes, you did the right thing. You were aware, and then you drifted off. That time is gone. As soon as you become aware of that unawareness, you're back on track. One meaning of mindfulness is to remember to turn toward the object of your attention. In this case, it is the whole-body breathing. This is why we call it a practice: it takes patience, persistence, and genuine interest. You wake up, you fall asleep, you wake up, you fall asleep. Everyone moves at her or his own pace. The ones who benefit from practice, as I've said before, are the ones who do not get discouraged. As usual, the instructions are simple: begin again.

Remember, too, that many of you have strong conditioning that says relaxation impairs alertness and that alertness is accompanied by tension. Gradually, you learn that a relaxed mind can also be extraordinarily alert.

* * * * *

Q: *I was taught to observe the subtle sensations at the nostrils. Whole-body breath awareness moves to a much more open awareness of breath, but I still find myself observing strong sensations that arise in the nostrils.*

A: Here's one suggestion. When you learn a new skill, especially one that is similar to one you've done in the past, you face hurdles. Previous methods can be powerfully conditioned into consciousness. Please remember that I am not imposing this on you. Rather, I suggest that you hand yourself over to it for a limited period of time.

Give whole-body breath awareness a try. Maybe you'll like it, maybe you won't. In the past, you set up house in the nostrils and that's where the breath is most vivid. Your mind said, "I like it here," and you moved in. If you decide you prefer this former technique, the nostrils happily await your homecoming.

• • • • •

Q: *By "moving in," I bring deep concentration to a particular breath sensation and observe its changing nature. But I also see the benefit of whole-body awareness and find I go back and forth between the two. What would you suggest?*

A: You mentioned that you watch the changing nature of the breath. That brings us to the fourth foundation of mindfulness: insight into the impermanence of all forms. You can observe this as you watch the breath emerge, exist, and disappear. You can use any object to learn about *anicca*, or impermanence. It is an excellent practice, though right now, it's not what we're emphasizing. Can you wait for a fuller answer when we take up the second contemplation?

I know many of you have worked with the breath in various ways. All sixteen contemplations are important. But throughout the literature everyone agrees that this one is particularly important: "Being sensitive to the whole body, the yogi breathes in. Being sensitive to the whole body, the yogi breathes out." At the same time, no consensus exists on the meaning of these words. My own teacher, Ajahn Buddhadasa, interpreted them to mean just at the nostrils. When I told him that his understanding made no sense to me, he laughed. He didn't care. And I don't care, either.

If you find that breathing at the nostrils helps you get calm and concentrated, and you don't want to try this new-fangled stuff, that's fine. I am all for what works. However, I want you to understand the advantage of whole-body breath awareness—and you can learn this only by putting the approach into practice. So I'll repeat it again: rather than emphasizing the power of a very focused mind, this approach emphasizes awareness of changing fields.

· · · · ·

Q: There's a neuroscientist who writes about Zen and brain plasticity. He does not recommend breath awareness for people who tend to be in their mind a lot—like I do—because it's a method that stimulates cranial nerves. Do you agree?

A: You may be interested to know that the ancient texts state the opposite: because breath has no content, it is not feeding the intellect. But forget about the ancients, forget about the neuroscientist, and forget about me. Just remember that this style of teaching is not a rigid system. It emphasizes flexibility.

Perhaps after giving whole-body breath awareness a good try, you will realize that it tends to stimulate too much thinking. Fine. Some yogis who think too much about natural breathing do not want to give up the more formal method of breathing taught in the *Anapanasati Sutta*. If that's the case, you can give the mind some thoughts to nibble on (for example, counting, or using the words *in* and *out*) to transition to the unadorned mindful breathing.

Over time, as you experience different methods and teachers, you will come to know the approach that is most fruitful for you. It needn't be a question of method X versus method Y. The basic instruction is just to be yourself, right here and now, sitting, breathing, and learning.

WALKING MEDITATION AND THE FOUR POSTURES

Whatever posture you use is up to you, but stay focused on the breath continuously. If your attention lapses, bring it back to knowing the breath again. Whatever you're doing at any time, watch the breath with every in- and out breath and you'll be developing mindfulness and alertness—full body self-awareness— at the same time you're being aware of the breath.

—UPASIKA KEE NANAYON, *Pure and Simple*

Since the time of the Buddha, alternating the postures of sitting and walking have been considered the most effective structure for formal meditation practice. So far, I've focused attention on the sitting posture only. Now let's expand the framework to include walking meditation, and also the postures of standing and lying down. I'll continue to focus on the approach of whole-body breath awareness, but please keep in mind that as you move into the other two phases— breath-as-anchor and choiceless awareness—that the guidelines you follow for sitting will also apply to your walking meditation.

I am quite certain that when most of you hear the phrase "walking meditation," instinctively you see a body, or a group of bodies, proceeding silently at a snail's pace. There is a good reason for this image to come to mind. When vipassana first reached the West in the 1970s, it was practiced in two forms, one from Thailand and the other from Burma. The approach of Mahasi Sayadaw of Burma was initially more popular, and it included styles of walking meditation that all emphasized making very slow movements. The main instructions were to move the body slowly and mindfully, accompanied by mental notes such as "lifting, moving, placing."

Such slow, careful movement is an invaluable method and lends itself to highly concentrated and precise seeing. As a result, most practitioners have come to think that walking meditation consists of unhurried, small steps. From the earlier days to the present, without verbalizing it, "slow" often is equated with "spiritual." Conversely, a fast or even natural pace is "worldly." After all, if everyone walks

at a natural pace during a typical day, how could such familiar ordinary movement be spiritual? Only dramatic, deliberate slowness,
so distinct from how you normally move, qualifies as a special and
genuine meditative exercise.

Or does it?

When I was on a three-month Zen retreat in Korea, occasionally
we sat for fifty minutes, and then someone banged the clapper. On
hearing that sound of two pieces of wood smacked together, we immediately rose up from our cushions and mindfully ran for ten minutes. When the clapper sounded again, sitting meditation resumed.
This alternation between sitting and rapid movement continued for
varying periods of time.

In Thailand, meditators often mindfully walk back and forth at
a natural pace along a path of twenty to thirty paces, reciting a man-
tra such as "buddho"("awake!") or contemplating a theme, such as
death awareness. When the well-known Thai forest master Ajahn
Chah visited the Insight Meditation Society in Barre, Massachusetts,
and saw for the first time a huge crowd of retreatants walking very
slowly, Mahasi-style, he stopped a few yogis and said, rather sym-
pathetically but also with a naughty, mischievous look: "I hope you
heal from your illness and can go home soon."

In another variation learned when I practiced at Ajahn Maha
Boowa's forest monastery in northeast Thailand, I was told to put
my right hand over the left in front of me as I walked, rather than
swing my hands or keep them behind my back. This was good advice
to emphasize a clear determination to focus the mind on walking.

But when I teach walking meditation, I encourage the natural
arm motion of swinging the arms at your sides, just as you might do
on an ordinary stroll. Why? Because I feel that it is crucial to convey
the message, even in small ways, that a stroll can be a fine dharma
practice if accompanied by sensitive alertness. This is all part of a
challenging program to help each yogi's practice grow from an idea
and technique into a genuine way of life.

Can you see that slow is just slow? Natural just natural? Even fast
just fast? It is the quality of mind accompanying the movement that

makes walking at *any* speed a dharma practice. Ask yourself, Is the observing mind present as the body goes from here to there?

As you walk at a natural pace, whether in the meditation hall or at home, you extend into movement what you do on your cushion or chair. The instructions remain the same: you inhabit the whole body with awareness, as best you can, and feel the breath sensations wherever you feel them. Here, too, you practice the art of allowing. The body is relaxed, and as the breath flows naturally, you receive it wherever it makes its presence known. Learning this relatively simple practice of walking at a natural pace with full attention previews the countless ways mindfulness practice can be brought into every aspect of life.

On retreat, I encourage yogis to walk at a regular pace, perhaps slightly more briskly than at home or in the street. It is definitely not walking slowly. The point is to just walk, which sounds easy enough. What could possibly interfere with that simple and effortless movement? Typically, of course, it is thoughts and emotions that enter the picture and separate you from intimacy with your direct experience of the breathing body in movement. Just as on the cushion, the mind has complete license. It is not restricted by time or space. It is shameless, and will do whatever it wants.

To an outside observer, you may present a beautiful image of a person who appears fully attentive while on the move. But it is a good bet that as you walk around the meditation hall, your mind suddenly starts kicking in with thoughts and plans. Perhaps you wonder what will be served for lunch, or what phone call you forgot to make.

When that happens, your practice is simply to come back, again and again, into that wholeness of full engagement with the activity of walking mindfully. Often, the breath sensations can be very subtle and the mind needs to become more refined or it will drift off and get caught up in thoughts or emotions. If that happens, see the mind separate itself from the activity of walking and go somewhere else. Don't get into a struggle. You are not at war with thought, or with any productions of the mind.

In the process of seeing that you are not fully present, the seeing usually corrects it. Then you are fully present again in the movement of your body. Here, as in sitting, intimacy cannot be forced; it comes about through seeing its absence. Just gently help the mind reenter the breathing body and movement, again and again and again.

If you practice this form of meditation with a group, you need a little energy to pay attention to the person ahead of you. But otherwise, your attention is inner, just as it is when you walk alone. This is not a time to suddenly become an interior decorator, fascinated with the design of the meditation hall; or a fashion designer, interested in everyone's outfit; or a botanist, attentive to the ferns and plants around you.

As in all forms of practice, the key is to stay awake. Awareness is never limited to a particular time, place, or posture; and neither is the breath. Wherever you find yourself, the breath is present. If you aren't breathing, you're dead. Mindfulness, the breath, and movement are happening within the same time frame. Can you be simple and alert enough to know this unitary event just as it is?

As you become more conscious of the body, the body thanks you. You become more connected so that the mind and body are whole, rather than the mind going in one direction and the body in another. In daily life, I have found that when I walk, it has become quite natural for the mind to be alert and aware of the body's movement, even if I am simultaneously talking to a friend or catching a bus. I have the same experience when I walk in a natural environment, such as in the woods or on a country road. Actually, the body enjoys intimacy with this activity. It is a healthy, sane way to live. You're more alive when body and breath are permeated with the energy of awareness.

Of course, every method of walking meditation has its benefits and limitations. One valuable slow walking practice I learned in Soto Zen instructs you to raise the foot on the inhalation and to lower it when you exhale. Breath awareness stays in synch with the walking. This precise, deliberate movement, like other slow walking techniques, enhances concentration and can be especially useful when the mind is restless or overactive. But it does not transfer well into daily life. If you doubt this, try slow walking on the street or at work—you may be escorted to a psychiatric ward or police station. The strength of the natural walking, by contrast, is its simplicity and naturalness. Since you walk in your everyday routines indoors and out, it is a form that transfers easily to life outside the meditation hall.

Some years ago, I learned a simple and extremely useful practice from Ajahn Mum, a Cambodian meditation master. He was, to put it mildly, an earthy teacher. When I first met him, I asked if he was a forest monk—"forest" often a code word for a true contemplative rather than a scholar or someone concerned mainly with rites and rituals. He looked at me intently, knowing full well what I was up to, stretched out his legs so that I could see the soles of his feet, and said: "All the forests of Thailand and Cambodia are imprinted on these feet." We both laughed and worked harmoniously together for the next two years.

At a later point, I asked him about a practice called "evening out the postures." I had erroneously understood this to be a practice of enacting each of the four postures—sitting, walking, lying down, and standing—for the same amount of time. First he laughed, and then he taught me the essence of this approach to mindfulness by suggesting that I do a retreat for one entire day moving through each posture. Rather than following a fixed amount of time, however, he told me to work intuitively.

I followed his instructions, and it was wonderful. The time allotted was not according to clock time, but to me. This meant that I might stay in a given posture, such as sitting, for an hour. Then I walked for ten minutes, stood for twenty-five, and laid down for fifteen. For a full day and evening, I continued with this practice, with time set aside for eating and bathroom needs. Within each cycle of the four postures, I varied the amount of time devoted to each one.

Why did I shift from one posture to another? I could not help but see my intentions and motivations. Was I being skillful? Lazy? Was I trying to escape from a painful emotion about to surface?

I realized that mindfulness is independent of posture, time, situation, or place. It was *always* available. Always. How liberating!

Ajahn Mum's teaching profoundly deepened my understanding of breath awareness in the service of waking up to every aspect of being alive. It has allowed me and many others to realize that meditation can be a way of life, not simply a collection of techniques reserved for special postures and places designated as "spiritual."

What do you do in each posture? Right now, you practice with whole-body breath awareness. Later, you practice the postures with breath-as-anchor and choiceless awareness. As your practice ripens and matures, your approach is fluid: sometimes you will use the breath for steadiness and calm, sometimes you will drop the breath entirely as you move at your own pace through each of the four postures.

When standing, I suggest you close your eyes. For some, this might cause a bit of shakiness or even anxiety, so experiment until you find the right way to arrange your legs and body weight so they are evenly distributed. This will enable you to establish a posture that feels stable and balanced. At the same time, remember the breath is unfailingly available to you as a friend and anchor. In the lying-down posture, you may find a strong tendency in the beginning to fall asleep. With practice, the body will learn to be totally relaxed in this position while the mind remains wide awake.

As part of self-discovery, you may find certain postures more fruitful than others. Some of you are more inclined to sit, and so you will sit much longer while going through these rotations. Others will find the walking more beneficial. All of the postures have a role to play, but their contribution reflects your individual nature. And of course, your choices will change over time.

Dear yogis, take a morning sometime and rotate intuitively through each of the four postures, using whole-body breath awareness (and later, also breath-as-anchor and choiceless awareness.) When you are distracted, just come back to it again and again. It is a formless and invisible practice with no dependence on a special location. I hope that this profound discovery, which has meant so much to me and to many other yogis, will help as you transform from a life that is largely conditioned and unexamined to one that is fully awake. Remember, *Buddha* means someone who is fully awake, alive and free. Imagine: A simple, familiar walk can wake you up!

2

Breath-as-Anchor

In Buddhist meditation, looking deeply is based on nonduality.
Therefore, we do not view (for example) irritation as an enemy
coming to invade us. . . . Thanks to this approach, we no longer
need to oppose, expel, or destroy our irritation. When we practice
looking deeply, we do not set up barriers between good and bad in
ourselves and transform ourselves into a battlefield. . . . We bring
the light of awareness to it (our irritation) by breathing in and out
mindfully. Under the light of awareness, our irritation is gradually
transformed. . . . the energy of irritation can be transformed into
a kind of energy that nourishes us.

—THICH NHAT HANH, *Breathe, You Are Alive*

IN THE FIRST MODE of whole-body breath awareness, you give exclusive attention to breath sensations. As your ability to attend to the
breath becomes more stable, intimacy with the body and breathing
emerge and bring the mind to greater calm, clarity, and peace. Confidence and conviction in the truth of the Buddha's teaching starts
taking root. The mind is now more fit to take up the second aspect
of the condensed method: learning to see insightfully, or vipassana
meditation.

As you begin this second step, the breath remains an anchor, a
support. Make it a light one, not one that you're rigidly tied to. Just

as in the first contemplation, you relax while at the same time remaining alert. Aside from the breath, this second mode of openness has no agenda—except what life presents.

Remember, you have been learning to allow the breath to flow naturally without imposing a model, form, or ideal on it. Now, with the same *art of allowing*, you open to your own life, your own experience, and watch everything reveal itself. As you sit, the entire mind-body process displays itself from breath to breath, and you watch it all arise and pass away, come and go. You are learning to refine the art of seeing, which is nonreactive and equanimous—a clear mirror that accurately reflects whatever is put in front of it.

Can you learn to welcome everything that emerges, whether a desire to shift your posture, a memory of a heated exchange with your partner, or even silence itself? Because you are used to specific goals and projects, many of you will feel uncomfortable just sitting with whatever arises. When that happens, simply see what is there: discomfort. When you wish for the teacher to give you a specific directive, then see the yearning—not the words, but that quality of the yearning mind.

All human beings experience the same mental states that come and go, come and go, but you're learning to relate to them in a particular way: you are awake to them without judging, interpreting, or explaining.

These instructions for the second mode are very gentle. But they are also ruthless. There's no such thing as a distraction, because whatever happens—that's *it*. The same emotions that you see in your sitting meditation—whether peaceful, anxious, or full of doubt—provide you with the perfect materials for practice. What arises will vary from moment to moment. The breath, however, remains constant. Even when a powerful energy such as loneliness or agitation visits, the breath remains present. Perhaps it is in the background, quietly, *in-out, in-out,* while your awareness is mostly involved with loneliness or whatever it is that has naturally captured your attention.

In this method, you take advantage of the breath's constancy.

It is such an obvious fact, and yet one that most of us often forget. Here is the Burmese monk Webu Sayadaw teaching this message to a group of his yogis:

> Sayadaw asked, "Don't all of you breathe out?"
>
> "We do, sir," they responded.
>
> Then Sayadaw continued, "When do you start breathing in and out?"
>
> "When we are born, sir."
>
> "Do you breathe in and out when you sit upright?"
>
> "Yes, sir."
>
> "When you're walking?"
>
> "We do breathe in and out then, too, then also, sir."
>
> "Do you breathe when you're eating, drinking, and working to make a living?"
>
> "Yes, sir."
>
> "Do you breathe when you go to sleep?"
>
> "Yes, sir."
>
> Finally, Sayadaw asked, "Are there any times when you're so busy that you have to say, 'Sorry, I have no time to breathe now. I'm too busy.'"
>
> The monks answered, "There isn't anybody who can live without breathing, sir."*

Of course, it is a truism that none of us can live without breathing. But can you make use of this truism, so that it helps your contemplative life? As you sit and use the breath as an anchor, it allows your attention to be more panoramic and open. It helps keep you awake, fine-tune your attention, soothe you, and cut down unnecessary thinking. Later, I'll discuss how a time might come when your contemplative life no longer uses the breath as an anchor. This is the third step to awakening, an approach I call choiceless awareness.

---

* From Webu Sayadaw, *The Way to Ultimate Calm: Selected Discourses* (Sri Lanka: Buddhist Publication Society, 1992), pp. 80–81.

Right now, however, if you choose to practice the second step, the breath will deepen and sustain your journey to wisdom.

This art of sitting with open attention is not easy to learn. It asks you to look at just what is there. Most of you have spent a lifetime *not* wanting to look at a lot of what is present in your life. You hear a meditation teacher say, "This is wonderful. This is how you get free." The words are inspiring, but despite your best intentions to sit and practice, you find that you resist this method of meditation.

I guarantee that as you sit in this mode, you will not welcome all the physical and emotional states that arise. Especially if you are new to the practice, you might resist looking directly at forceful ones such as throbbing pain, or grief, or fear. That's fine. You sit on your chair, bench, or cushion, switch to this second mode of openness, and find you can't do it. You try, but the mind gets cloudy and con-flicted. It endlessly analyzes, psychologizes, and thinks about what comes up. You may go around in circles, lost in thought, dissecting what happened at work earlier in the day and what might happen later in the evening.

At other times, what occurs in the mind—maybe memories or emotions—becomes overwhelming. Because the quality of your at-tention may not yet be at a point where it can meet these mental activities in a useful way, you become overrun by them. At times, you feel as if you might drown in them.

In both cases, whether you are caught up in thought or over-whelmed by emotion, it can be wise to go back to exclusive atten-tion to the breath and practice the first method, whole-body breath awareness. Part of developing meditative skill is for you to know what you can and cannot take on. Should an emotion such as loneli-ness come up and you're not ready for it, then you bow to it: "Thank you very much." But know what you are doing. It is not denial or repression. Rather, this response says, "Whoa. This is a tidal wave of loneliness, or of thinking about loneliness. I can't handle it right now." At that moment, it's fine to just go back to the breath. *In-out, in-out.* Maybe finish up the sitting that way.

Sometimes when you go back to the first method of whole-body awareness, you need only a few breaths, and the mind settles down again. Then it gracefully returns to the field of free attention and, accompanied by the breath, you are able to stay aware of mental and physical states as they arise and pass away. But as you know, in this practice you can't rest on your laurels. During your next sitting, you might take the same number of breaths and find yourself drowning in agitation or remorse. Everything is just what it is in that moment. Unfortunately, no buzzer goes off and indicates, "You're now ready for vipassana." Knowing when to do this is an aspect of self-understanding. I can only give you a rough guideline; once you get there, it's both artful and pragmatic. Even if you could practice easily with open attention the day before, and then find you cannot do it at all the next morning, it is wise and skillful to return to the first mode of whole-body breath awareness.

Here, I want to add a few words of caution for all of us on this path. Sometimes practitioners say to me, "OK, I hear what you're teaching, but I think I need two or three more years before I can look at rage and loneliness and all those heavy emotions." But if you indefinitely postpone the practice of open attention, you run the risk of never developing it at all. Taken to its extreme, this might mean that if you switch too quickly away from the painful states that inevitably arise, you strengthen habits or patterns that avoid observing the mind in the present moment. And if you never look at what's happening, you are never going to get free of it. Even concentration on the breath can be misused as a high-class avenue of escape.

In other words, when you use only the first method of breath awareness, it can temporarily put you in a more peaceful state. But if you limit your practice to this method, your quality of life doesn't substantially change, because you're still not dealing with the source of your suffering. Vipassana practice is a wisdom practice that emphasizes liberation from the root of suffering in the psyche. This uprooting is borne out of the accurate seeing of things exactly as they are.

Do you recall that in the first method, I emphasized the arts of allowing and receiving? There, you were learning to let the breath occur without force or control, and to remain fully present to receive it—not to grasp or scurry after an "ideal" breath. By developing this attitude of allowing and receiving the breath, you also were preparing the mind to more skillfully relate to far more challenging arisings, such as anger or fear.

At the same time, let me repeat, especially for beginners or for those of you in the midst of troubling times: when faced with a highly charged emotion or endlessly repetitive thoughts, often you might need to go back to the first step of this process, which is exclusive awareness of the breath. This is understandable. Even after full enlightenment, the Buddha himself set aside personal retreat time for the practice of mindfulness of breathing, calling it "a joyful abiding in the here and now."

As you sit and breathe, you practice the first of the four foundations of mindfulness, or the first *satipathanna*: mindfulness of the body in the body. Often I describe this more succinctly as cultivating intimacy with the body and the breath, without judgment or analysis.

Now let's bring the practice of whole-body breath awareness to the second foundation of mindfulness, which looks at *vedanas*, the Pali word for feelings or sensations. In this teaching, the vedanas are not synonymous with emotions; rather, they are the pleasant, unpleasant, or neutral sensations produced by immediate contact through any of the sense doors. In the Buddha's teachings, there are six sources of contact with sensory life or feeling: seeing, touching, hearing, tasting, smelling, and the mind, which is also considered a sense door.

In parts of the Buddhist texts, the vedanas make the world go round. When something is pleasant, there's a tendency to want to grasp it, hold onto it, or desire it to come back. This is what happens when you take a bite of chocolate cake, push away the plate because you do not want to eat anymore, and then find yourself sticking in your fork for one bite more, and then another. Finally, you polish off the entire portion. This lack of awareness of the vedanas often drives you to compulsively seek more and more pleasant feelings.

Your response can be similarly compulsive or mechanical when you are unaware of unpleasant sensations, only now there is a tendency to distance yourself from or obliterate them.

A few years ago, at a retreat I led in a rural setting, workmen repairing an old building filled the air with the din of saws and hammers. The yogis were furious. Many had carefully saved their money and rearranged their lives to attend. Understandably, they desired a bucolic atmosphere, with the low hum of insects and the songs of birds. As complaints increased, I checked with the office. Then I told the group that members who wished to go home could get their money back. Those who remained could choose to use these unexpected conditions as a practice.

No one left the retreat. I suggested that yogis pay attention to the unpleasant sensations that arose on hearing the sounds, and to its accomplices, annoyance and aversion. With careful attention, many yogis began to see that the mind's reaction to the sounds was related to, but distinguishable from, the sounds themselves. When heard with a clear and accurate mind, the sounds were simply *bang, screech, clomp.* For many of the retreatants, unpleasant sensations thinned out and even fell away, allowing the yogis to be at peace with simply the way it was: *bang, screech, clomp.* Fortunately, the repairs were short-lived. But the practice of "in the hearing, just the hearing" profoundly affected many throughout the entire retreat.

Finally, in the second foundation of mindfulness, there are the neutral sensations. Often, when you experience these, there is a tendency to fall asleep or fill the mind with projections or other mental fabrications. Many of you do not realize how much of your life is neutral. You think nothing is happening. But something is happening: a neutral feeling. Test this in your own life and see what happens when you notice this. Does the mind tend to fill up time and space with a juicy fantasy or plan or worry?

When you sit and breath mindfully, pay attention to your whole body and, at the same time, to sensations that immediately seem vivid or distinctive or neither. Then see if these are pleasant, unpleasant, or neutral. Don't spend a lot of time deliberating. Just note your obvious, initial reaction. Bring awareness to that part of the body. Perhaps you are aware that your right ankle feels slightly taut, giving rise to an unpleasant feeling. Or that your hands feel relaxed and soft, and that pleasant sensations arise. Feelings and sensations of this kind happen constantly. But only when you pay attention during meditation do you enter a slightly different dimension and become attuned to whether that sensation is pleasant, unpleasant, or neutral in the body. As you notice, for example, the feelings in your ankle or your hands, it might change and become less intense. Or it might not. Wherever the sensation resides, know if it's pleasant, unpleasant, or neutral.

When your awareness of the vedanas is weak or nonexistent, it can set in motion a chain of events that lead to craving, aversion, or delusion. That's why the teachings often refer to them as the weak link in the chain of causation. With practice, as you become more fully aware of a feeling at the moment it happens, this awareness diffuses the energy of the vedanas. It breaks the link between feelings and the aversions, cravings, and delusions that lead to suffering.

There may be periods in your sitting practice when you can look carefully and develop awareness of these sensations or feelings in the breath, or what is called *vedana upasana*. Often the in-breath and out-breath each have dramatically different feeling tones, whether pleasant, unpleasant, or neutral. As I've suggested, just being with the breath as it becomes more continuous can bring a feeling of peace and even rapture. The breath sensations can be smooth and soft, and spread a warm flow throughout your body: lovely. The trouble begins when you become attached to them. Frequently, if you fixate on pleasant sensations in the breath and elsewhere in the body, you want to make them a permanent home or at least extend their life. But what happens when the "expiration date" runs out and you expect the next sitting to be filled with even greater peace than the previous one—and then can't even find your nostrils? Suffering!

At other times, the breathing can be so unpleasant—fighting its way in, fighting its way out—the mind resists paying attention to it.

As you sit with this obstreperous breath, you tell yourself, "I don't like looking at this. This is not a calm, joyful meditation session." Now the challenge becomes seeing if the mind can remain steady, fresh, and clear even in the midst of highly unpleasant sensations. The breath, which you have been using as an anchor, has become the problem.

Some practitioners assume that to meet this challenge, they need to learn a new technique or method. But that's not the case. The message remains the same: see the aversion and also see the absence of equanimity. You come to equanimity by regarding awareness of the breath exactly as it is in the moment: non-equanimous. Seeing this offers you the valuable understanding that the mind is able to become aware of its own limitations. In other words, awareness sees it is being colored by aversion, craving, or ignorance. Accurate seeing emerges from inaccuracy. At this point, you're back on track.

More and more, by strengthening awareness, you're able to receive whatever happens in a nonreactive way. The mind learns to remain clear and firm even in the face of oscillating sensations, whether pleasant, unpleasant, or neutral.

Please keep in mind as we move through the four foundations of mindfulness that I am discussing them in a linear style. Language, especially written language, has its limits. It imposes a sequential order that is not necessarily mirrored in reality. Your experience on the cushion or chair will not be so neat and tidy, and your practice will not move in lock step from the first through the fourth foundations. Often, each of the foundations of mindfulness arises at the same time. The instructions are to work with whatever appears most vividly, moment to moment, and to keep developing a steady and accurate mind that remains with what life presents. Understanding the limits of language on the page will lend more fluidity to your practice.

Now let's turn to the third foundation. As you sit and breathe, you look directly into the mind without judging the quality of mindstates that arise and pass away. Here, you are learning a fundamental teaching of the Buddhadharma: to familiarize and investigate the *kilesas* and their absence. *Kilesas,* or the three mental poisons, are greed, hatred, and delusion, and all their variations.

Let's say a torrent of fear comes up. Remember, it's not the word *fear* that visits you, but the actual energy you label *fear.* The energy is experienced in the body and through the entire nervous system. The pulse changes, breathing itself changes, posture changes, the mind changes. Everything is tinged by fear.

When this energy of fear arises, it seems as if it will last forever. It can feel as large, unmovable, and permanent as a mountain. But as you look closely at fear, the energy changes moment by moment. Perhaps fear peaks. Then it begins to dissipate. Sometimes it erupts again. The pattern of fear is not consistent or predictable. But eventually, with mindful attention to this mental state and with the breath as an anchor, the energy thins out.

Mindfulness, awareness, attention—these are also not merely words but forms of energy. When you are mindful, when you notice fear and shine the light of awareness on it, the seeing-energy meets the energy of fear and transforms it. Breath by breath, as you practice this way, fear falls away.

It is all the shifting dynamics of energy. The powerful energy of awareness transforms the energy frozen in the form of fear. Then that energy is released and free and available to you. An ancient image from the Chinese Ch'an tradition likens the ordinary mind to ice and the awake mind to water.

As you continue to sit, using the breath as an anchor, more and more you experience a radical change in your approach to life. Perhaps for the first time, you see that you're no longer helpless in the face of mental states that inevitably arise. You have what you need to meet whatever challenges life brings. You have come to know from direct experience that when once-terrifying emotions surface, they are workable—even if seen, at first, as immovable mountains. And the reason they are workable is because they are *observable.* You are looking directly into the mind.

With practice, the quality of that observation and attention can become like an unwavering flame, stronger than anything that comes in front of it—including the energy of your biggest fears. As I'll describe in a later chapter, this transformative practice is not limited to formal meditation. It carries over into every moment of your daily life. Of course, confusion or fright or annoyance may still come up in your sitting practice. But if it does, it is far more benign. The day might come when you greet anger, say, with an attitude that simply says, "Oh, here comes anger." It's far less overwhelming because it is accompanied by awareness, which extracts much potency out of the energy. At that point, anger becomes a tiger that has grown weak and has lost its teeth. You know the tiger is angry, and that's OK.

Many years ago, I worked with Sayadaw U Pandita, using the Burmese method of making mental notes for everything that happened during formal meditation. My mind became very, very clear. I would start to make a mental note and the words would fall apart. I went to Sayadaw and said, "I remember to make a mental note but as I start to make it and I hear it, it's just nonsense. It just decomposes." He became very happy. He said, "Great," and asked, "What do you learn from that?" I felt confused and couldn't answer. So he filled me in: "That thought is empty, insubstantial. You see the true nature of thought."

Observing and understanding the nature of thought is another aspect of the third foundation of mindfulness. As you practice vipassana meditation, using the breath as an anchor, you come to see that thoughts hold fierce power over you because, like anger and fear, you identify with them. Take a simple thought that new meditators experience so often: "I am a rotten meditator. I am no good. I am hopeless and will never be able to train my wild mind." Well, if you make "hopeless," you have "hopeless." Don't make anything! That is best of all.

Or perhaps as you sit, you produce a thought about enlightenment: "I'm light years away from it. It can't happen to me. Everyone else in the meditation hall, but not me." When that thought comes through, often you believe it and identify with it. "Yes, it's true. I'm worthless. I'll never be enlightened." Instead, pay attention to the thought, and see that a thought is just a thought. Did you know that? That's all it is. It is as solid as skywriting.

As you continue to practice, you observe thoughts that arise, just as you observe strong emotions. You come to know that thoughts have no intrinsic power. You perceive their empty nature. Even the most repetitive and compulsive thoughts, like powerful emotions, will eventually weaken and fall away.

At first, though, you cling to your thoughts—and find that they can take you for a quite a ride. But if you don't get discouraged, the wisdom you develop begins to discern the difference between when you are riding on a train of thoughts and when you are standing on the platform, watching the train pass by. As your mind settles, try this method: "In this sitting, as I breathe in and breathe out, I'm just going to watch my mind do thinking."

In the light of awareness, thoughts fall apart. More and more, you live from that place of clear seeing rather than a place that gives total authority to the realm of thinking. This is a giant step toward freeing yourself.

• When you come to the fourth foundation of mindfulness, with your minds and hearts more trained in awareness and understanding, you look at the heart of the Buddha's teaching, the Dharma. Here, you're benefiting from emergence of insight to see into the lawfulness of impermanence and letting go, or *anicca;* its close cousin, not-self, or *anatta;* and the suffering that inevitably comes from not seeing these truths, or *dukkha.*

As you sit with the breath, open to everything, you realize that life is composed of changing forms. Seeing into the changing nature of all forms—*all* forms—has profound significance to your practice of vipassana meditation. You see the law of impermanence at work, independent of content: at work in the sitting body, at work in the mind, at work in the universe. Apparently, this is the way life is. More and more, you come to see that thoughts come and go, the body is in constant flux, no mood stays forever, and attitudes oscillate, just like the weather. You're happy, you're unhappy; you're optimistic, you're a naysayer. It's too noisy, it's too quiet.

In some Buddhist monasteries, offerings of flowers placed on the altar are allowed to wilt a bit—and often, far more than a bit, because not immediately removing them provides a teaching. What happens when you see the impermanence of a freshly picked flower? One reaction might be to vow to never buy a fresh flower again because it dies on you. Another is to purchase plastic or silk flowers. But a better alternative is to enjoy the delights of the beautiful white azaleas or mums while they are alive. You know how to do that. You don't fall on the floor gnashing your teeth and screaming about the loss of the flowers. You've learned to enjoy them while they last, and to understand that when they're gone, they're gone.

As you develop insight into impermanence, even starting with something as simple as a flower, over time it extends to what you might call the big stuff in life. All of you will age. You will grow ill. You will die. Needless to say, you have a hard time with that. It's not flowers—it's *you*. But as you build an understanding of change and insubstantiality in the world around you, you begin to observe a natural law at work in your actual person. It is not an intellectual concept. In fact, true insight has no thinking in it. It is a direct experience that becomes bone deep, with no separation between what you know and what you are.

As your practice of sitting and breathing helps you see everything arise and pass away, perhaps it helps you become more comfortable with the naturalness of change and the fact that you are very much part of nature. No one is singled out. This clear and accurate seeing of impermanence helps you understand one of the Buddha's most precious teachings: it makes no sense to attach to anything in an unstable and uncertain world. To grasp or hold on only results in a head-on collision between what you want to be and how things actually are. In other words, it causes suffering. As you see this, you come to know the freedom of letting go of attachments. Dear friends, I hope with all my heart that your practice leads you to this source of true inner happiness.

Not long ago, a student reported that as he contemplated the impermanence of his own life, he realized that he longed to change his career from that of a computer technician to one that would be more socially useful. As this yearning grew, he felt tormented by confusion over the precise nature of his future direction.

In terms of practice, this experience of uncertainty could be translated as "*I* am confused." But our practice is not to be confused by confusion. Rather, it is to see it as a self-centered mind-state. The old mind that has generated the confusion is attempting to solve the problem that it has created. The only hope of an authentic solution is through the freshness of clear seeing. A calm, steady mind is in a far better position to answer the question about changing careers—or any question that comes up. Remember, no one has to be confused by confusion! Confusion is simply a mind-state. Awareness is never confused: it is a clear mirror that reflects the confusion but is not distorted by it.

To his great relief, this student understood the teaching. Though he still felt uncertain about his vocational path, the added burden of "confusion" fell away.

Will he remember this clarity if confusion reemerges in a future sitting? Unfortunately, most of us lose or forget it. Instead, the mind insists that "I" am confused. The more you identify with it, the more potent it becomes. You think, "This decision about my future over-whelms *me*." As you identify with the confusion, you also strengthen the sense of *me*, of *my* self. Your mind and body amplify a sense of *me* who is puzzled and distressed. Perhaps this involves experiencing yourself as a helplessly mixed-up meditator.

Once again, you're back at the process of self-ing, or me-ing. This cannot be reiterated often enough, because, finally, this attachment to *me* and *mine* is the core source of suffering, according to Buddhadharma. You all know how to do this because, like most of the human race, you identify with nearly everything that happens to you. As you sit and breathe, you identify with moods, even as they swing wildly across the spectrum from happiness to despair. You identify with self-images, from that of top-ranking scientist to inadequate parent.

To me, the ultimate renunciation of contemplative practice is when you renounce this tendency to identify with everything as

being *me* or *mine*. My family. My identity as a holy person. My out-
rage and passion for justice. My vegetable garden. Everything is so
personal! Typically, in religious circles, renunciation means giving
up things such as sex, money, excessive food, and possessions. But
these external practices are not ends in themselves; they are designed
to help you reduce your tendency to spend your lives self-ing. It is
possible to live in a monastery with only one meal a day and to still
be an egomaniac. Similarly, it is possible to own an extensive ward-
robe and live in an elegant home and be free. I witnessed a living
example of this when I practiced Zen in Korea. From time to time,
an elegantly dressed, highly successful attorney, with a family, visited the monastery. He bowed to the monks and they bowed to him.
Alert, happy, and affectionate, he was considered to be and treated
by all the monks as an authentic Zen master.

You have to understand what you're all up against. Self-cherishing is brilliant and incredibly subtle. In this respect, you'll never run
into anyone shrewder than yourself. There are roughly seven billion
"self-ers" living on earth, with many more on the way. That's one
reason why the planet looks the way it does. It's amazing that we're
still here at all!

Seeing the lawfulness of impermanence, not-self, and suffering that
underlie the entire mind-body process allows you to meet life as it
is—and to meet yourself, exactly as you are. This direct experience
gains increasing depth, as you attend fully to whatever you encounter because that is your life in this instant.

The act of taking care of the present moment possesses a dynamic energy that gradually and naturally moves you in the direction of full awareness. Sitting and breathing and knowing. Enjoy the
show (though at first you may not). See it come and go, arise and
pass away, appear and disappear. It's quite a production.

The degree to which the breath helps you settle into mindfulness is invaluable. But don't become a breathomaniac! That would
be missing the point. As I will discuss in the next chapter, what matters is that as your practice develops, your home becomes awareness

that watches and sees everything, It watches and sees even the reluctance to sit and do the practice of anapanasati, or any practice at all. That's not a problem. One moment, you will be so enamored with formal meditation that you map a journey to Thailand to become a monk or nun. Ten minutes later, agitation flares and you think, "Forget Asia. I've got to get out of here and order myself a large pizza."

Most of you know these extreme shifts of feelings toward practice. They do not disappear. What does change is your relationship to them. As your awareness develops, aversion to the practice becomes just as welcome as devotion to it. When a yogi recently complained about distractions during her sitting meditation, and told me that this made her feel like shit, I said, "What's wrong with shit?"

Don't be at war with anything that arises in the mind. But if you are, you have the perfect material for practice: the agitation and dynamism of inner warfare.

A time may come when you find that you don't make the split between the first and second steps of whole-body breath awareness. Many great teachers see the distinction between samatha (a concentrated calm) and vipassana (insightful seeing) as artificial—though invaluable at various times in your practice. As the Ch'an master Hui Neng said in the *Platform Sutra*: "Shamatha and vipassana are like a lamp and its light. If there is a lamp there is light; without a lamp there is darkness. The lamp is the body of the light; the light is the function of the lamp. The names may be two, but in essence they are basically one and the same."

Let me end this chapter with the story of a yogi who showed me the profound suppleness of the steps in the full awareness of breathing method. Sadly, this yogi suffered from an advanced form of cancer of the throat. She started out using breath-as-anchor, following the general instructions that I've taught in this book, only to realize that her natural interest in the impermanent nature of breathing offered her the most valuable approach. So we remained with step one and custom-tailored it so that her entire focus was on the unstable and changing length and quality of each in- and out-breath. In other words, though step one is most often used as a samadhi practice, it can also be one of insight or wisdom. This heart of vipassana, or insight—awareness of the impermanent nature of all forms— became the yogi's dharma door as she simply used the in- and out-breath to see it at work.

Because she was so close to the end of her life, and her practice of seeing impermanence had stabilized, I suggested that she engage with an extremely challenging practice: the *Maranassati Sutta* ("Mindfulness of Death"). After an initial bout of terror, she became able to observe the breath while reflecting that her life literally hung in the balance: if there was no in-breath after an out-breath, she would not be alive. This intense practice yielded wisdom and peace before she died. I'd never before worked with anyone else in this manner and have not done so since.

As you see, the two-step method of mindfulness of breath is limited only by the level of creativity of you and your teachers. It is designed, like all meditation, to help you use your experiences and understanding in a way that serves you and serves life. It helps you develop an attentive mind that's keenly interested in learning how to live and how to die with wisdom and compassion.

Eventually there is no "you" doing the seeing—it is just seeing. The seeing-energy becomes like a flame that removes the potency of whatever is in front of it.

* * * * *

Q: Even though I felt very calm when I came into the meditation hall, as soon as I sat down on the pillow, my breath was unsteady and I began to feel a wave of anxiety.

A: Remember that you're not trying to fit the breath into a particular pattern or rhythm. The breath is simply the way it is. You're using it as an anchor now, to help look at mental states, such as anxiety. Most people understand breath as a technique only for calm and concentration, but you are practicing with it to help pay attention to whatever arises. The Buddha taught awareness of breath to help insights flourish as well as to quiet the mind. Because the breath is constantly with you and accompanies you every step of the way, it can help you open up to life and see your reactions to everything you encounter.

* * * * *

Q: Can you clarify the distinction between becoming focused and concentrated, and the broader practice of mindfulness?

A: At times, if you concentrate exclusively on one part of the body—say, the nostrils—you become so absorbed in the body and breathing that you don't hear the traffic outside. Some teachers and students are drawn to these states of absorption. At the deepest level, they are called the *jhanas*. In some approaches, they are classified in stages, and often include states of joy, peace, and bliss. The deeper you go, the longer distractions abate. The mind becomes more clear, stable, and strong. But in these absorptions, afflictions that disturb the heart go into abeyance only temporarily; once you "come out" of the *jhanas,* there they are, patiently waiting for you.

This is not the direction emphasized right now. You're heading toward vipassana, which is a wisdom practice. Wisdom engages a broader experience of your full life and understands how to uproot the sources of suffering. Of course, an adequate level of calm is essential—but it needn't be as concentrated as the absorption practices.

Here's a famous teaching story from India that illustrates the distinction you asked about. An ancient king was both an exemplary secular ruler and master yogi. Seeking to understand this unusual combination, a subject asked to study with him. The king said yes, and then instructed the man to put a pot of hot oil on his head and go through every room in the palace without spilling one drop.

The man completed the task and reported his accomplishment. "Wonderful!" said the king. "Now, can you tell me what's going on in the palace—political intrigues, coups, sexual affairs, assassination plots?" The student replied that he was too concentrated on not spilling a drop of oil to observe the world around him. So the great king said, "Now put that pot of oil on your head, walk through the palace, don't spill a drop, and tell me what's going on."

. . . . .

Q: After I use the breath to reach a fairly strong steadiness of mind, do I then use it as a background for everything that comes up?

A: As you investigate the approach of whole-body breath awareness, I suggest that you keep the breath in mind. Of course, in this second step, you loosen your grip on breathing and use it as an anchor to help steady attention. With breath and awareness happening at the same time, you carefully watch the mind-body process and the rise and fall of all forms.

But the decision is not arbitrary. It is artful. More and more, you have to guide yourself. Let's go back to the example of anxiety. Suddenly, you sit on your cushion or chair and the breath is unpleasant and even difficult to find. Don't struggle to capture the breath sensations. Remember, there is a distinction between focusing on the breath, as suggested in the first step, and this second method, which is to be aware of the breath as you focus on what vividly happens in the moment—in this case, anxiety. It's possible that the breath may not be at all accessible in a given moment. No problem: it will enter your field of awareness again.

If you drop the focus on the breath and look directly at the anxiety, you might find that awareness can flourish without using the breath as an anchor. Perhaps ten minutes later, you can return to the breath, and it will help you investigate the nature of the anxiety.

Neither choice lasts forever. As you practice these two steps—or for that matter, any number of different methods—eventually you learn to develop confidence in your ingenuity and intuition. With patience and honesty, you will choose wisely—based on what works for you.

. . . . .

Q: I find that when I'm agitated, the mind cascades out of control. But if I'm upset or anxious and pay attention to the breath in the body for only a few moments, it brings the awareness into the body and really changes my emotional response.

A: Yes, that is what it is designed to do. Think back to the discussion on the *Kalama Sutta*—this is what it pointed to. You're learning the benefits through your own experience, not borrowing from the Buddha! You discover that as you become more embodied in the present moment, you're less caught up in the onslaught of feelings or mental states. In effect, you short-circuit the mind's fantastic imagination and its ability to place you in an alternative reality.

Also, you come to know the body from the inside, as a field of energy. You grow more sensitive to it. Our enormous intelligence in the body has been stunted because we have misused or neglected the body. Whole-body breath awareness and also using the breath as an anchor helps you develop more intimacy with your body, and this is beneficial for your physical health as well as for insight practice.

. . . . .

Q: When I was sitting just now, very concentrated, a tremendous wave of sadness came over me. I wanted to get rid of it by going out to take a walk on this beautiful day.

A: Welcome to the human race!

. . . . .

Q: So I stayed with the sadness and it passed. But I felt tremendous aversion to it.

A: That's fine. This practice has endless nuances. In pure observation, you see the aversion as a reaction to the sadness. Awareness helps you see and learn that when you look at a mental state in order to get rid of it, the quality of the seeing is compromised. Aversion is a *kilesa,* an emotional affliction that clouds awareness unless you see it as it is happening.

Here is one suggestion. If you keep labeling something "sadness, sadness, sadness," the word itself may become a powerful conditioner. Like throwing kerosene on a fire, it creates a conflagration. So throw out the word and just look at the energy of what you call sadness. Experience it in the body as you breathe in and out. Feel the more subtle expression of it in the mind. If the word appears, observe how the mind manufactures a label or verbal explanation for what's happening. That label is not neutral, like the label on a jar of orange marmalade. Certain words, such as *fear* or *loneliness* or *sadness,* carry strong judgment and power. Try wordless seeing—what we're calling *clear seeing.* It has no purpose other than the seeing itself. You ask for nothing in return. Nothing comes next. Just this.

· · · · ·

Q: Recently, I dreamed that my dying father was already laid out in a coffin. When I meditated today, the feeling of panic at seeing him there returned. Before this happened, meditation was peaceful. Now I am afraid of what might come up while I'm quietly sitting.

A: Start by looking at this fear-energy, and at the same time, know that your old friend the breath is always right there to help you. Of course, you all want to feel peaceful and happy. You can choose to carry the pot of oil on your head through the palace with a calm demeanor. But if you choose to go in the direction of wisdom, it will require that you learn to fully look at your life as it is from moment to moment. Meditation is like your life. Sometimes great joy and happiness fills you, sometimes great disappointment and fear. It will simply show you what is there.

· · · · ·

Q: Can you tell us in greater detail how to deal with fear? It comes up again and again for so many of us.

A: This is a case where it helps very much to practice in a group, because you encourage one another to do what normally you would not want to do. At a certain point, you will see that fear, or worry, or even grief over the death of a loved one are not bad. Why? Because they are part of the composition of life.

Try to examine fear with fresh eyes. You will see that the mind doesn't want to cooperate. It says, "I can't stand this!" Sometimes you see that fear grows like a plant in the soil of thoughts about the future. But here's a radically new attitude: Fear is part of life, part of the natural world. It's not weird or invasive. It's similar to thunderstorms, trees, and earthquakes. Remember in the Buddha's teaching, nature and mind are one. When you take an interest in all life, including fear, you bring awareness and clarity to it—and tremendous energy is released.

You are learning how to turn toward the fear. It is a new and challenging skill. Most of you spend a lifetime trying to avoid certain mental states. But tremendous energy is squandered in your unexamined fears, aversions, and escapes. When you open to them, that trapped energy is released. Life becomes more spacious. Can you imagine how much of life is distorted because you haven't faced fear? How much creativity is cut off because you're afraid you will fail?

. . . . .

Q: *When difficulties come up, using the breath has a calming influence. It helps me sit more easily with painful feelings. So I am bringing a goal to this process: using the breath to feel better. Does that undermine my practice?*

A: Please don't be so hard on yourself. You described a skillful use of breath. It is calming and it can help you walk into the valley of afflictive emotions. It is skillful, healthy—and legal! But you're right: strictly speaking, it is not a wisdom practice, because when you do not deal with what's happening in the present moment, you cannot become free. Concentration puts you temporarily into a more peaceful, clear, and happy state of mind. Insight uproots the problem.

You need to investigate whether going back to the breathing is a recurrent way to avoid unpleasantness—or is it a "tactical retreat"? To use a military metaphor, a good general knows when to retreat so the troops can acquire dry clothing, rest, and hot food, in order to be more effective when they return to the front. As a meditator, you are the general, the troops, and the enemy! Your choice of method is an art, not a science.

I'll repeat the caution I mentioned earlier: like any concentration technique, the breath can be used as a high-class means of escape. When you become very experienced, it can be like pushing an elevator button. Here comes terror: switch to channel breath. When this happens, it means that you haven't dealt with the fear—it has only gone into abeyance. But let me also repeat: whether you use it to calm down or to help investigate mental states, conscious breathing is a tremendous ally.

· · · · ·

Q: Could you help me find a starting point for dealing with the intense anger that arises when I am sitting on the cushion?

A: Some people will say that if your anger is so fierce and overwhelming that you can't look at it, then bring in antidotes, such as loving-kindness. Or return to a focus on the breath. But the approach I am teaching in this second contemplation, as you know, urges you to be aware of whatever turns up, using the breath as an anchor.

When the energy of seeing touches the energy you label "anger," the anger loses its potency. You break the identification with the "I" who is outraged or attacked. You renounce the tendency to identify with the anger. Rather than *I am angry,* you begin to see that anger is arising. It is an element of nature, of human nature, just like loneliness or happiness. When you see this, you remove the toxicity of that emotion.

This is the wisdom practice I've been sharing with you throughout this book: direct seeing. You are learning how to use the breath as an anchor to help you remain steady and calm in the storm of even the most tyrannical mental states. Be prepared to occasionally get washed ashore and blown away. But in time, mindfulness can become like a flame that is stronger than whatever is in front of it. Through your practice, it is a skill you can learn.

. . . . .

Q: *So if the anger comes up, you just sit there and look at it?*

A: You don't *just sit there.* You bring total, full attention to the anger. There is no separation between it and you. You experience it fully, without pushing it away.

But I don't want to make it into a formula with means and ends: if you look at anger, then you succeed in getting rid of it. I have to use words, but in the actual practice of pure seeing, there is no motive except the seeing. That is its potency. If you aim your attention, as if it is a laser beam designed to destroy the anger, then your motivation weakens the power of direct seeing.

. . . . .

Q: *But I thought you said, when the feelings come up, stay with the sensations in the body and do not give thoughts or words to them. Am I confused?*

A: A little. Lay aside the word "anger" or "fear" or whatever. Look at the energy, not the word. People talk about locating the energy in the body. But it's not just there. It's also in thoughts and emotions. Remember, the Buddha's teaching is about the entire mind-body process.

. . . . .

Q: *So when you talk about clear seeing, it can include thoughts, visual imagery . . .*

A: Whatever is there. The content doesn't matter: it's the quality of the mirror-like seeing. It includes the body and the full realm of human experience. The point is to not feed the thoughts or feelings or get entangled in them. When you do, you're no longer meditating—you're thinking or analyzing. You're all experts at chronic introspection. In the deepest insights, there's no thought. None. It is just clear seeing. A mind at peace can be empty or contain some thinking—the stillness remains intact.

· · · · ·

Q: I can be quick-tempered. I had an argument with a coworker, and it kept coming back to me, night after night, while I meditated. Eventually, I understood my role and my mistakes. Meditation seemed to take the venom out of the encounter. Is that part of insight meditation?

A: What you did is fine, because the experience ceased to be a source of suffering. You didn't feed it. This is a form of reflective insight, which is the skillful use of thought. Let's say an event is over and the damage done. You and your colleague fought it out. Through meditation, you experienced insights into your behavior. Perhaps you felt remorse for hurting a colleague. As you practice, you might begin to see that this is a habitual style of relating, and no longer useful to you.

You admitted a mistake, felt regret, and used your reflection as an occasion for learning how to live. If you can't acknowledge mistakes, how can wisdom emerge and flourish?

However, this is not the deepest understanding of vipassana, which means clear, deep seeing. As your ability to see clearly strengthens, you find that you rely less on any kind of thinking, even useful reflections of this kind. Clear mind is a form of nonconceptual intelligence that can respond wisely to a given situation, at the moment it arises.

3

Choiceless Awareness

. . . .

Letting go of form is trusting in the immediacy of awareness. And awareness is real. It isn't abstract; it isn't just some kind of concept I have that I don't recognize immediately; it is more like the space in this room and the forms in space. They are what they are. And I no longer go from one thing to another saying, "I like this; I don't like that," but recognize that whatever is in this space belongs here at this moment. It doesn't matter whether I approve or disapprove of it, or whether it is good or bad. If it is here, this is the way it is; and this is learning to trust in awareness, which doesn't pick or choose. It is choiceless awareness.

—AJAHN SUMEDHO

IN THIS CHAPTER, we will explore the immense significance in formal sitting when you no longer use the breath as an anchor, but instead "focus continually at the mind pure and simple," as the Thai meditation master Upasika Kee guides us to do.

But why drop the breath now, when I have given it such a prominent role in these writings so far? What would it mean to abandon the breath and "only" look directly into yourself?

In the earlier methods in chapters 1 and 2, you've seen how whole-body breath awareness enables the mind to calm down and stabilize itself. As the body becomes more comfortable with the flow of breath energy and feels more "planted," it is able to sit for extended periods of time. As you observe it with greater continuity, the breath calms down; since the breathing conditions the body, the body also is more inclined to relax. You have "attained a seat," a more stable physical abode from which to observe and examine the entire changing nature of the mind-body process. You do this with no judgment or analysis of what turns up in the mind. As you practice this mode of openness and free attention, you also rely on using the breath as an anchor.

In my own formal meditation practice, after years of benefiting from this approach of breath awareness, again and again I came to find myself in a mind that was spacious and silent, empty and at peace. This mind, free of concepts and highly charged with subtle life energy, was startling—and totally new to me. To intentionally continue to direct attention to breathing seemed extra and unnecessary.

It was not a matter of dropping the breath. More accurately, the breath dropped me. If the breath could speak, it might have said: "You can continue to use me as an anchor if you like, but it isn't really essential, is it?" As the effort to be mindful dropped away, a more natural course of action seemed to be *nonaction*. Gradually, I engaged in the practice of recognizing and stabilizing this discovery, of resting in it and allowing it to work on "me."

Why did I do this? Why should any of you? Are we now done with breath awareness? Have we strayed from Buddhadharma? After much reflection, and at times, anguish, I realized that for me, this was a natural fulfillment of everything that had come before. It was a unique expression of a dharma inheritance that included many great teachers, teachings, and years of practice. More and more, this flame of awareness became my home. The love of seeing and of learning from what has been seen, both internally and externally, was all the inspiration I needed. To this day, it remains true.

But please understand that my experience does not portray an inevitable arc of practice. This approach to meditation does not prescribe a rigid trajectory. Given my many years of wholehearted commitment to anapanasati as a complete dharma practice, dropping the breath as a support of awareness was an intense, highly questioned, and somewhat dramatic process.

In addition to learning from my own investigations, over the years I heard from many other yogis who practiced full awareness with breathing and arrived at a similar conclusion. Of course, each came to this decision in a unique way. For most, it was a natural progression, not a studied curriculum.

I emphasize this because the teachings offer an abundance of methods that use the breath. Most students of vipassana enter the Dharma through the door of mindful breathing, which is also the common form in many other Buddhist meditations. Often, mindful breathing is limited to a simple, natural way to develop samadhi—concentration—and then dropped. But as explained in previous chapters, for those who practice anapanasati, the breath is also used to develop both calm *and* insight into the arising and passing away of all forms. Some practitioners, probably a far smaller number, closely follow the guidelines of sixteen sequential contemplations in the *Anapanasati Sutta*, which use conscious breathing as part of a path leading to full awakening.

Remember the obvious fact that as long as you are alive, the breath is with you. Of course, that includes when you practice sitting meditation, no matter the approach you use. At times, for me, breath sensations are quite vivid, for the simple reason that they have received years of special attention! And in particular situations, I deliberately turn to breath awareness. When I am ill and in bed, for example, I attend to the first method, whole-body awareness of breath, for it seems to foster the healing process. Also, as I'll explain in the next chapter, often I will use breath awareness in the course of daily life. Now and then, if my mind is unusually busy, I will take a few moments of breath awareness to calm and ready it for choiceless awareness.

When you drop using the breath as an anchor, and practice with mindfulness as your sole refuge, you enter true choiceless awareness. In this way of inhabiting the present moment, there is no agenda or prearranged object to attend to. From moment to moment, whatever turns up plays a vital role, whether it is contact with awareness, bodily life, sounds, or smells. Nothing is left out.

There is also the quality of nonjudgment, which includes not picking and choosing, not approving or disapproving what the mind encounters. There are no interpretations, explanations, or analyses.

Sometimes ancient masters called this *mirror mind*. I referred to this image in earlier steps as you used the breath to help develop the art of clear seeing. In choiceless awareness, the method develops without an object of focus, or an anchor. The Japanese Zen master Bankei, whose teaching emphasized naturalness and spontaneity as a corrective for overly formalized ways of practice, described it beautifully: "A mirror reflects whatever is in front of it. It is not deliberately trying to reflect things, but whatever comes before the mirror, its color and form are sure to appear. Likewise, when the object being reflected is removed, the mirror isn't deliberately trying not to reflect it; when it is taken away, it doesn't appear in the mirror." In other words, the mirror does not try to grasp or capture the image when its time is up. It has no ideas about what should or should not be next. In choiceless awareness, this mirror-like mind does not cling to what it longs to preserve or push away what it dislikes.

In the second step, breath-as-anchor, you practiced openness, with no agenda, so you are familiar from that approach with the art of sitting on the cushion, receptive to what life itself presents. But now, without the breath as an anchor, perhaps it is even more tempting than in the previous one to ask: "What now? What do I attend to when I sit down to meditate?"

My answer, once again, is to tell you that I cannot answer your question. I haven't the slightest idea. Life itself sets the agenda!

All of you must learn to let this happen. "Agenda setting" has a lifetime of practice; its momentum is formidable. Now you are encountering an entirely new skill—or perhaps, another stage in the "art of allowing and receiving" that you developed in the first two methods. Whatever you encounter in here-and-now is your life, until it disappears, and then you encounter what arises next. And next, again. You are mindful only of what, in fact, is already here. Why? Because it *is* here. You allow life to do the choosing for you. Your practice is choiceless, with no deliberately selected content and no object of direct or indirect attention, such as the breath.

Often, when yogis express confusion about what to attend to, I suggest that choiceless awareness is akin to listening to a classical symphonic orchestra. Multiple sounds from a vast range of instruments appear simultaneously. If you listen carefully, however, sometimes the sound of one instrument, or one section of the orchestra, dominates. Sometimes you hear the notes of a single violin or cello, only to soon hear a mix of sounds blended together again. You hear what you hear: perhaps beautiful and soothing melodies, perhaps cacophonic and unpleasant ones. If you play the piano, or the drums, you may quite naturally be attuned to those sounds. Perhaps, as you listen, you catch a moment or two of silence.

At times, your attention at a symphony may be comprehensive and all-inclusive of the orchestra, and at other times, narrowly focused on a single instrument. The same holds true as you practice choiceless awareness: the key is to remain awake as it all unfolds. Can you enjoy the entire show?

Clear, accurate seeing is an art: the art of pure observation. How do you dust off the mirror, so that it sees accurately? A vital part of your practice is to look in on the quality of mind that is doing the observing. The Buddha's teaching emphasizes the three poisons of the mind—greed, hatred, and delusion—that powerfully and often unremittingly color your view of yourselves and others. In the practice of choiceless awareness, you see these blemishes in the mirror, and by seeing them, they are weakened. Remember, the energy of seeing thins out the energy of everything it touches, even the potent energies of the three poisons. Each of you has the potential to use awareness to weaken them, and even wipe away all the dust, moment by moment.

It is in choiceless awareness that I find myself most at home in my practice. A particular discourse of the Buddha, called the *Bahiya Sutta* (*Udana* 1.10), continuously serves as an inspiring guide for this approach. When Bahiya, "the bark-clad one," desperately and insistently pleaded for a liberating teaching, the Buddha responded by saying something along these lines:

> Then Bahiya, you should train yourself like this: In the seeing there is only what is seen. In hearing there is only what is heard. In sensing there is only what is sensed. In thinking there is only what is thought. Then Bahiya, "you" will not exist; whenever "you" do not exist, you will not be found in this world, in another world or in between. This, just this, is the ending of suffering.

The Buddha teaches that when your mind regards experience simply as it is, without adding anything to it, you are not defined by what you experience. There is no "you" in relationship to that experience. In fact, there is no sense of "you" at all. All of conditioned experience is just seeing, hearing, smelling, tasting, touching, and thinking. Eventually, there is no "you" doing the perceiving. It's just *seeing*. Total attentiveness. The seeing-energy becomes like a flame that removes the potency of whatever is in front of it. Or as my Zen teacher Seung Sahn Sunim summed it up: "Don't make anything!"

As this practice of choiceless awareness develops, the mind opens up to a level of consciousness that's beyond thinking. It's prior to thinking and has infinite depth. All the stillness and inner peace you could ever want is within you already. It's in each of you. But comfort and confidence in it comes only as your practice develops. Often the word *silence* is used to describe it. *Silence* is an unassuming word, easy to misunderstand. It is also inadequate, because it attempts to describe something that is wordless. Once again, we're working within the limits of language. The Zen saying, "Open your mouth and you're wrong!" totally applies here. But we have to do it anyway—as attested to by the voluminous writings of Zen masters!

Everyone has a different reaction to the word *silence*. Many of you are wary of it. Sometimes, since you are so unaccustomed to silence, you devalue it. Or mistake it for vacuity. You can't help thinking it is a waste of time or a break from "real" living. After all, you've been brought up planning, doing, getting, going. That's what fuels much of conventional life.

But please do not be misled by our culture's neglect of the need for life's contemplative dimension. Silence is a highly charged, subtle, and refined form of existence. Unquestionably, it is vast and teeming with life. For some, this very spaciousness can be frightening. When you experience this fear, you might find that the mind tries to figure out what this silence is all about—just as it has spent its life figuring out everything else. Such mental effort or analysis is the kiss of death. It kills silence, because how can *thinking* understand the *absence of thinking*? The thinking mind concludes that silence is where it is not, and reclaims its position there.

Should you find that the mind naturally enters into silence, can you allow it to work on you, without analysis or reactivity? Just rest in the silence.

Today, for most people, silence happens when the TV goes off, the refrigerator stops humming, and the house is quiet. "Whew. Finally. I can just sit and have a cup of tea." Perhaps you sense it in the evening on a quiet city street or country road. Certainly, it occurs when you visit places where no one speaks, such as retreat centers. But as many of you have experienced, even in a place that is totally silent, the mind can be hectic, wild, and filled with noises of vexation and fear.

Inner silence, even in a meditation hall, develops slowly. Scientists tell us that this level of silence may happen when you fall sleep and enter the dimension called *dreamless sleep* or *profound sleep*. Why is it so quiet in that time and place? Because the big noisemaker—the problem maker, *you*—isn't there. And that's why you feel refreshed in the morning.

All of you possess the ability to tap that quality while awake. Meditation is designed to take you to that place; perhaps we should call meditation the process of *falling awake*.

Learning about this silent mind is one of the primary elements of learning how to live, the skill more commonly referred to in Buddhist teachings as wisdom. Though impossible to truly name, each tradition has many names for this state: silence, the original mind, our true nature, Buddha nature, original wakefulness, enlightenment. Sometimes enlightenment is called *the great silence.* Once again, there's no adequate word or phrase for it. Often I like to use the term *engaged stillness,* because it's a reminder that the silent mind is not reserved for the meditation hall. It is recognized, appreciated, and nourished there, of course, but it also flourishes through its engagement with the world.

Many concentration practices help you open to the stillness of a silent mind. The Buddha offered and encouraged these practices, such as the *jhanas,* as methods to reach deep inner states. From my own experience, I know that this practice of deep absorption can bring extraordinary peace and joy, and greatly benefit contemplative life. Some people are particularly gifted in this concentration practice, and it is used by masters and students alike.

But it is not the approach that I am encouraging you to practice right now. The practice of choiceless awareness does not develop the stillness of a narrowly focused, concentrated mind. In that state, the mind becomes absorbed in its own silence; temporarily, all mental fabrications go into abeyance. But engaged stillness engages you in the fullness of your life as you actually live it, whether on the cushion or chair or in your daily life.

As you tap this very refined, vivid form of life that I call silence and engaged stillness, you may develop a love for it, even a passion for it. More and more, as you practice choiceless awareness, it is possible to live in and from it.

The depth of silence that I'm talking about is present right here, right now as you read these words. It lives very deep in the human heart. It is also incredibly shy. If you want it, it runs away. You can't think your way to it. You can't feel your way to it. You can't command it or demand it or plan how to get it. But if you love it, if you're open to it, it becomes eloquent and tremendously healing and helpful. How to get to this silence? Not by trying to get to it, for that only brings frustration and disappointment.

Silence is hiding in your heart. It doesn't want to be bossed around or told when to show up. Like anything else, with practice you can learn how to surrender to the silence, so that silence is just silence. You're not using it to get somewhere else, not even to diminish suffering, although great healing occurs when this silence is activated. I've observed that when I emerge from extended periods of dwelling in this form of silence, I am kinder to others. This is not an intention when I practice. It just seems to be a natural by-product. To my surprise, others have noticed this even before I have.

You reach silence by clearing away the brush, clearing away your preoccupations that are so deafening that you don't even know the silence is already there. It's intrinsic to your nature. As you continue to practice the art of observing, watching thoughts come and go, moods come and go, the mind empties itself of its own content. You find yourself in the silence that's always been there.

As all the thoughts, and likes and dislikes, all that you think of as being *me*, fall away, even just for a minute or two, you discover what's inside you. During some formal sittings, this awareness extends well beyond a few minutes. It can even become, at times, your home. You see that it's something vast and silent and whole. You see that it's not up there or out there, but that you are "it."

Silence, or engaged stillness is our great untapped resource. Without it, you're not living anywhere close to your full potential. But as practice continues, more and more your life emanates from this place of clear awareness. When the seeing gets very clear and still, it is because "you" disappear. The great Chinese poet Li Po expressed this beautifully:

The birds have vanished down the sky.
Now the last cloud drains away.

We sit together, the mountain and me,
until only the mountain remains.*

---

* Sam Hamill, trans., "Zazen on Ching-t'ing Mountain," from *Crossing the Yellow River: Three Hundred Poems from the Chinese* (Rochester, NY: BOA Editions Ltd., 2000).

Li Po did not rise up and leave the mountain scenery. His self-conscious mind has left him! He is describing a mind that has stopped churning out ideas, thoughts, feelings, and images. In his case, you might say that he no longer exclaims, "Look at that gorgeous view. I'm so happy to be here. I can write a poem about this scene, and it will be remembered forever. Perhaps even anthologized."

None of that chronic mental activity remains. His poem implies that self-cherishing has fallen away, and what remains is simply clear seeing.

· · · · ·

Q: *I'm still trying to understand more clearly what you mean by the terms engaged stillness or choiceless awareness.*

A: Let me share a story told to me by Aoyama Roshe, a wonderful Zen teacher and tea master with whom I spent a few hours when she visited the United States. When Aoyama was a young nun in Japan, the abbess of her monastery once said, "A nun's mouth should be like an oven." At the time, Aoyama understood that sentence as instruction to follow the monastic tradition of eating whatever is given. When the mouth consumes food without discrimination, it is like an oven or furnace that burns up everything thrown into it, whether high-quality logs or thorny branches.

Only later did she realize that the abbess was instructing on a deeper level: the "mouth" of one's life. She was teaching her students about sitting in open awareness. Yes, the furnace consumes whatever is put into it. But it also creates heat and thermal energy that allows people to cook their food and to keep warm. In other words, it transforms wood into beneficial elements.

As I've said before, *awareness* is not just a word. It is a verbal designation for a quality of extremely refined seeing-energy. It has no weight or color and you can't grab it. Yet as the observing mind becomes more potent, it is like the oven. When the seeing-energy touches the energy you label *fear*, or *loneliness*, a beautiful alchemy happens.

Vipassana meditation is the practice of gradually widening your capacity to receive, without judgment or preferences, whatever turns up. You are with it because it is there; nothing is discarded or trivial. You're learning to become intimate with all the wood that's thrown into the oven. Being fully with what happens in the present moment, a liberating transformation happens. That's what makes it a dharma practice. This is choiceless awareness at work.

Now, to get to the term *engaged stillness*. I coined this term to describe how it is possible for the mind to be still and clear—in other words, open awareness—even in the midst of the verbal and physical action you encounter in daily life.

.   .   .   .   .

Q: *I am not a newcomer to meditation. But I wonder, What I should do in my practice if I cannot experience the great silence you talk about?*

A: Just take care of the present moment. This is it. Watch the mind to see what is actually happening, not to acquire what you think *should* be happening. As you experience life in the moment, the day may come when you find yourself in silence.

These instructions and methods are designed to help you to allow this to happen. I understand that if you have not tasted a semblance of this silence, you may feel disappointment or frustration. Unavoidably, we dharma teachers supply new ideals, and from these, new forms of attachment and striving might emerge. We give you a new form of suffering! If that happens, you will move in the wrong direction. Better to let life unfold and be awake and present in the midst of it. You will not be disappointed.

Clear seeing sets in motion a natural dynamic. It is self-knowing in action. If you find yourself suffering from spiritual striving or doubt, just look at that. After all, it is what is happening in the moment.

. . . . .

Q: You talk a lot about "self-knowing." Is this similar to the virtue of self-knowledge that philosophers like Socrates talk about—or is it a dharma term?

A: Self-knowledge often refers to an accumulation of insight and information. But in self-knowing, you are not encouraged to collect data or to write a book about yourself—a biography of your growth and insights. Quite the contrary. As used here, self-knowing is valid only in one given moment. You're learning how to see clearly and directly, and out of the clear seeing comes self-knowing. As the process becomes more refined, you can't separate the seeing and knowing.

Self-knowing is the gateway into wisdom and freedom. You do not store it away to use as the basis for seeing in the next moment, because then it would not be fresh. That's why note-taking during dharma talks or on retreats is discouraged. Just listen, or sit and walk, and know! Self-knowing occurs in the active present. That's its value. Period.

. . . . .

Q: Is it possible to reach a point of stillness or choiceless awareness, and still use intellectual thought processes?

A: It's a good question. Let me answer it a bit indirectly. Meditators have known for centuries about the brain's plasticity—that brain cells continue to grow throughout the span of your lives. They have known the truth of limitless mind, and that our commonly held notion of "life" is rather limited. Now the neurosciences are catching up and confirming that only a tiny fraction of your brain is utilized.

The mind that is clear—not lost in thinking—sees the same old world but not through the same old eyes. One of my deepest insights occurred when I was looking at a yellow cab. My mind was very quiet, and I found myself in tears. Suddenly, I discovered why they called it a yellow cab—because it was *yellow.* It was so yellow, my heart broke open with joy.

With meditation, you're opening to a new dimension of living. And you're asking me: Can you live in that place? Can that place of silence—prior to thinking—express itself, and can it infuse your actions when you need to think and talk and act? The answer is yes. But it takes practice and skill to learn to live there.

When I prepare for a dharma talk, I go into silence. For me, silence is better preparation than notes or rehearsals. I was trained this way by Zen Master Seung Sahn, who insisted I never use notes to teach the Dharma. Rather, like a jazz musician, I was encouraged to choose a theme and just "blow." Usually, this approach works, though not infallibly. Once, when I was giving a talk on the four noble truths, there was great freshness and spontaneity—but an omission of one of the truths. On another occasion, with about one hundred people in the hall, I attempted to give a talk without a prearranged theme. As I sat there for quite a long time, nothing came up—except anxiety. So I watched the anxiety, and it gave birth to a dharma talk on anxiety.

Please understand that I'm not suggesting you reject the exquisite qualities of mind such as the ability to think, investigate, analyze, or design. These do not disappear. But with silence, they can be infused with a changed energy.

Within the infinite depth of silence, words are irrelevant. However, if words are called for, they emerge out of the intelligence activated in the emptiness of inner peace.

* * * * *

Q: *Ideas and beliefs about rebirth are often mentioned in dharma books. I wonder if you could tell us whether you believe in rebirth.*

A: If you are a person brought up in a culture that has believed in rebirth for thousands of years, such as in Tibet or Thailand, the answer is obvious. I've known wonderful Tibetan teachers who look at me with sympathy when I say I'm uncertain about rebirth. On the other hand, many professors in the sciences might look at you like you're crazy if you even mention the subject. All I know is that I am open to the idea but honestly *don't know*! Do you believe in rebirth?

. . . . .

Q: I have no idea. It's far beyond me. Don't you feel anxious or frightened not knowing?

A: Not really. For me, the famous "don't-know mind" is a place of alive openness that I truly love. Here, not-knowing is not merely a lack of information but rather a receptivity to life as it teaches us how to live. Even some of the Buddha's students, thousands of years ago, shared our uncertainty. To those who lived a life aligned with dharma principles, the Buddha quite reasonably suggested two possibilities: if there is rebirth, they were in good shape; if there was no rebirth, they had upheld a well-lived life. Personally, I am quite comfortable with the Buddha's view of this matter.

Several years ago, life-after-death experiences were all the rage. As I listened, I asked the question far more vital to me: is there life *before* death? That's my bias. I have a simple understanding about the purpose of life. I believe life is here to be lived. That's it. Then the question becomes, "How?" To me, that's the singular question each of us must answer for ourselves.

. . . . .

Q: I have experienced benefits from becoming more calm and aware. But I look to expanding my compassion to other people, and that has not happened. So my question is, When does awareness give way to greater compassion?

A: There are two approaches to this question of developing compassion. One involves the steady cultivation of compassion, or *karuna*, which is one of Buddhism's four *brahmaviharas,* or sublime virtues. The other three virtues are loving-kindness (*metta*), sympathetic joy (*mudita*), and equanimity (*uppeka*). The use of certain methods to develop and strengthen these states is part of the historical teachings of the Buddha. Many contemporary teachers encourage practice with these methods. I have done intensive practice of all four, and found it profoundly beneficial, as have countless yogis.

The second approach is based on the teachings of the great Indian philosopher and yogi Nagarjuna—sometimes called the second Buddha. It stems directly from the Buddha's teachings, though Nagarjuna developed it centuries later. Perhaps you desire to amplify your compassion or loving-kindness, and it's not happening quickly enough to suit you. You yearn for it. In this approach, rather than pursuing the ideal of becoming Mother Teresa or Mahatma Gandhi, you observe the moments when you are like Stalin or Hitler. In other words, see clearly when you are harsh, judgmental, ungenerous, filled with ill will and even murderous rage. Or, observe your acute disappointment at your inability to relate with compassion.

Why? Because you do not acquire a quality by striving after it. Start with seeing its absence. Perhaps you speak viciously to your partner. Then you beat up on yourself and swear that you will become a kinder, gentler person. I suggest instead that you see how hard you are on yourself—because there's a high likelihood that you're equally hard on others. This is self-knowing in action. As it develops, you might find that compassion is right there, waiting for you. It's not something you have to cultivate and grow.

The first method described is a cultivation practice and the second is one of pure observation. But please do not view these two approaches in either/or terms or think one superior to the other. In this book, and in most of my teachings, I encourage direct observation and the learning that flows from it. But I also teach the cultivation of the wonderful human qualities practiced in the *brahmaviharas* when I perceive it will be beneficial to a particular yogi.

· · · · ·

Q: *Can you relate developing wisdom and compassion to the practice of choiceless awareness?*

A: Sometimes the Buddha's teaching is characterized as a bird with two wings: wisdom and compassion. In truth, they are one and the same—and they are inseparable! Wisdom is not genuine without compassion, and compassion without wisdom is dangerous. The

Dalai Lama uses the term "idiot compassion" to describe the attempt to be a "good person" without wisdom. Often this type of idealized goodness backfires and even causes harm.

When you enter choiceless awareness, or engaged stillness, it's quite mysterious: there is an organic intelligence in that silence. Maybe I'm deluded, maybe thousands of years of teachings have perpetuated this delusion for many Buddhists, but I've seen that this organic intelligence that grows out of silence includes what we call compassion and love.

Finally, meditation is an explosion of compassion and love. If you do not feel that, something might be skewed in your practice. I'm not talking about sentimental or romantic feelings. This love is a real and potent energy, a force in the universe as strong as death and as universal as the law of gravity. Your cultural conditioning takes a holiday. You make the remarkable discovery of what human life is all about. That's why people devote their lives to this practice.

PART TWO

Living Awareness

4

Awareness in Daily Life

•   •   •   •   •   •   •

Constantly watch over the mind as a parent watches over a child.
Protect it from its own foolishness, teaching it what is right.

It is incorrect to think that at certain times you do not have the
opportunity to meditate. You must constantly make the effort to
know yourself; it is as necessary as your breathing, which continues
in all situations. If you do not like certain activities . . . and give up
on them as meditation, you will never learn wakefulness.

—AJAHN CHAH

WE HAVE FOCUSED all our attention so far on the practice of awareness in formal meditation postures. But for most of you, this comprises only a small fraction of your life. Eventually you get up from
your seat and meet what awaits you—which is "merely" the rest
of your life. You raise children, attend classes, travel, and work late
hours. You come to know success and failure, you enter and leave relationships, you thrive in health and then suffer with illness. Nothing
is left out of the content of your here-and-now. Nothing!

Can the contemplative skills you have been learning help you in
the realm of daily experience? What part does conscious breathing
play in it all? Can moment-to-moment dharma practice blossom into
a way of life rather than remain confined to protected situations?

Of course, the answer is *yes*. Awareness and insight can develop anywhere you find yourself, from sitting on a bus to answering the phone to leading a global conference on the web. What matters is the quality of your mind and your interest in learning, not where you are. Yet if this claim is true, why come to places like meditation halls and retreat centers? And why devote time each day to sit in silence, developing practices on the cushion such as breath awareness and choiceless awareness?

I'd like to take a well-known teaching from the Soto Zen tradition and bring a vipassana yogi's eyes to it to see what light it sheds on practice in daily life. The teacher is Dogen, one of the great Japanese Soto Zen masters, and the lesson is called Dogen's "Instructions to the Cook." One of my own teachers, Katagiri Roshi, gave it to me many years ago, and I've found it extremely helpful ever since.

As a young monk, Dogen was not satisfied with what he was learning in Japan, so he took a trip to China to learn about Zen in that part of the world. When the ship docked in port, Dogen observed an elderly Chinese monk who had come aboard to buy Japanese mushrooms. On hearing this man speak to the captain, Dogen realized this was no ordinary monk.

As Dogen would soon learn, the monk was the Tenzo, the head cook of the monastery. In the large Chinese Zen monasteries, the purchase and preparation of food required arduous labor and tremendous skill. Clearly, the Tenzo had a mature practice. Eager to forge a friendship, Dogen approached and asked (I will paraphrase the conversation), "Can I get you a meal here and some tea? Let's talk over the finer points of Dharma together."

The old man said, "No, I haven't time for that. I need to get back to my monastery. There's a celebration going on and I want to add some Japanese mushrooms for the special meal that will bring delight to the monks."

Disappointed, Dogen said, "Oh, come on. You don't really have to do that. Can't you just stay and discuss Dharma with me?" Essentially, he was saying to the Tenzo, "You have a chance to share the Dharma with me and you want to go back and cook?"

Finally, the old monk said, "You really don't have a good understanding of Dharma, do you? You really don't have a clue." And he left.

The monk was telling Dogen that he had created, as so many of us often do, a split between what we call "Dharma" and what we call "daily life." What Dogen had learned from the cook was that practice and living could be the same.

The Buddha's earliest teaching likewise represents practice and life as one. It appears in the suttas when he makes a simple statement that is repeated many times: "Be mindful while sitting, standing, walking, or lying down." Earlier, I talked about the formal practice of these four postures. But it is easy to overlook their more pervasive meaning. The words may sound boring: *sitting, standing, walking, lying down.* Say something interesting! But your entire lives are lived out in one of these postures or in moving from one of them to another.

In these instructions, the Buddha tells you to be mindful throughout life. What I am saying is merely an extension or enrichment of this idea.

Historically, the men and women who first studied with the Buddha in the earliest years of his teaching in India were not living in monasteries. They wandered and lived outside, and the Buddha himself lived most of his life in the forest. Later in the Buddha's time, larger gatherings of people would come together to practice—but again, this was only for the duration of the three-month rainy season; for the rest of the year, they dispersed.

When the Buddha's teachings spread from India to China, at first the Chinese tried to do it the Indian way. But theirs was a different climate and culture. Though one emperor of China closed down monasteries and forced many Buddhist monks to disrobe, the Zen sect survived. One interpretation says that the Chinese spared Zen practitioners because they were more at home with them: Zen monks farmed, cooked, and cleaned. In the eyes of the earthy Chinese people, the other Buddhist monastic sects slacked off and expected others to take care of them.

Pai Chang, the Chinese monk who strongly influenced the rules governing Zen monastic life, said, "A day of no work is a day of no eating." If you don't want to work, fine—but you don't get to eat, either. Even in old age, close to death, he continued to go outside to work until it was time for him to die.

The Zen influence in China enlarged monastic life to include farming, cooking, and other labors. In time, it influenced Dogen. Given the conditions of monasteries in his native Japan, his encounter with the Chinese Tenzo served as a wake-up call for him to learn that everything you do—even cook or clean the kitchen—can be Dharma. Of course, Dogen's profound understanding is not limited to labors in the monastery. Its deeper lesson, for all of us, is about our entire way of life.

Most of you come to sitting meditation practice because you are suffering. If you were totally content and happy, with complete peace of mind, why would you seek out something like this? Once you find this peace, and especially if you start to see how valuable it is, you set aside time for it in a sheltered place, like a retreat center. And when you leave that special environment to return home, often it is the lingo of the retreat culture to say, "I'm going back into the real world."

I think this is a big mistake. There is only one world. Prior to all forms—vipassana, Tibetan, or Zen, or any school you could name—there is simply life expressing itself in multitudinous forms. These forms have been invented by brilliant human beings to help you live your lives with less unnecessary suffering. Is the particular form useful? Is it special? Absolutely. But it's also not special: it is an invaluable convention that brings people together to deepen their understanding and sensitivity

At the same time, remember that a convention such as a meditation or retreat center is not Disneyland. The challenge is right there, too. The environment is alive with yogi jobs and retreat meals and a room full of people, even in silence. But it remains a world arranged in a particular way to help develop certain qualities of mind.

For thousands of years, meditators have discovered that these qualities are more easily developed during a retreat or a formal sitting practice.

Many years ago, I arrived to teach at the Insight Meditation Society, in Barre, Massachusetts, earlier than usual. That was when I discovered that participants had arrived hours in advance to try to sign up for the softest yogi jobs. Apparently, this was a retreat tradition. The best job was to dust off the books in the library; the worst was cleaning dishes and pots, as no dishwashing machine existed at that time. This "tradition" surprised me, as I had taken for granted an approach to practice that placed tremendous value on any type of work needed to make a retreat center or a monastery functional. I learned this while practicing in Zen monasteries in Korea and Japan.

Because I have always believed that our approach to yogi jobs is pivotal to a robust practice for laypeople who live in the world, I instituted a "law" during retreats that I led: yogis were randomly assigned jobs, without the option to pick and choose (except for medical reasons). At first, this led to a few dramatic conflicts, such as the time an oral surgeon was assigned to clean the toilets. Despite the staff's skillful attempts to persuade him to accept this job, he adamantly refused, and so they sent him to me. We chatted, and when I drew him out, he was honest and direct. "Look," he told me. "I didn't go through all those years of schooling to come here and clean toilets. I find it demeaning to do that."

Not wanting to justify it too much, I simply said, "But that's our policy. If you don't do it, you have to leave the retreat."

He said, "Come on, you're kidding, right?" And I said, "No." I explained about developing a practice that would be of value to him well beyond the retreat. Finally, when he realized I wasn't bluffing, he grudgingly took on the job.

It turned out to be a success story—and has remained a minor legend at the retreat center. The dentist felt tremendous resistance for three or four days, because he found the job humiliating. But he watched his suffering, kept at it, and by experiencing those surges of emotions, he could directly see how cleaning the toilets threatened the image of himself he had painstakingly crafted. In that direct see-ing, a tremendous burden of his self-created identity lifted. By the end of the retreat, he was a joyful toilet bowl washer. He could have starred in a TV commercial.

This is the potency of developing a practice that infuses every element of life. It is gentle, relaxed, but also unrelenting. It keeps bringing you back to insight and awareness, again and again. So if you go on a retreat, I hope you are given a job you *don't* like.

I deeply value contemplative life. I love to sit and have been sitting for many, many years. Sitting meditation is special in that its utter simplification helps you calm the mind and cultivate insight and compassion. I've seen that if you fall in love with the sitting, you can get very calm. You can experience peace and joy. For those of you who haven't fully tasted it enough, you will. It's lawful. It's not reserved for special people. But once it happens, there's a tendency to become attached to it and prize it over and above the rest of life. For many, it can become an obsessive activity—and made to stand for "The Practice." This can easily happen because the central icon in Buddhadharma is a human figure, composed and serene in the sit-ting posture. You never see the Buddha vacuuming or making love.

In the very early days, when many of us went on long retreats, I noticed that we would come home from a three-month stint sharply aware of how precious and valuable it had been—but then spent the remaining nine months of the year earning money to get back to the next three-month retreat. Each successive retreat was worn like a combat ribbon.

A pattern emerged of dedicated yogis coming out of protected, special environments in this country or in Asia, and then returning to a world where there was no place to continue the practice. Seeing this pattern was one of my strong motivations in 1987 in founding the Cambridge Insight Meditation Center. I deliberately decided to make it a nonresidential center, because I wanted people to come to CIMC and then to go back home to families, or to schools or jobs, and test what they had learned in the fire of living.

Recently I learned, to my surprise, that a large percentage of high-ranked martial artists often fail to employ their skills under the stress of sudden attacks on the street. Though supremely accomplished in the practice hall, they lose their skillfulness outside a structured enclave. Meditators face the same challenge.

Let's look at something else that often happens after a retreat. Perhaps you have developed a wonderful samadhi: *breathing in, breathing out*. You feel at peace, you love the human race. Then you drive home, and as the mileage goes up, your hard-earned samadhi goes down. You stop for gas and check your cell phone. An unexpected text from your mother's physician and an angry e-mail from your next-door neighbor pop up on your screen. Samadhi vanishes and you experience disappointment at its absence. Maybe doubt arises, and dread of the days ahead, filled with deadlines and stress. If you remain mindful of these mental states, you are solidly on the path of practice. Isn't disappointment part of life for everyone? Without this mindfulness, however, you might begin to despair of both retreat centers and daily life.

My first teacher of meditation, J. Krishnamurti, started us off from day one with an emphasis on seeing life and practice as one thing—so much so that he dropped the word *practice*. Because I began with this understanding, I've never had to breach a gap between the formal practice and daily life. But though today's meditation culture often gives lip service to the belief that practice and life are the same, often it fails to put these words into effect. And despite my own understanding, I quickly came to realize that when I taught, often I inadvertently fostered this bifurcation. If I emphasized daily life, some people began to say things such as, "My practice is my three-year-old child who is my live-in Zen master"

And I would say, "That sounds good, but when was the last time you sat?"

Answer: "Let's see. I can't remember, it's been so long."

Me: "Right, because you have a live-in Zen master. I forgot."

In other words, the "daily life is my practice" notion can become a misguided cliché. My attempts to alter this pattern failed. If

I shifted my emphasis back to sitting, students' formal practice assumed center stage and daily life withdrew to the side. When I called attention back to daily life, it undercut formal meditation. For me, to this very day, the challenge in teaching is to stress the vital nature of daily life practice without undermining sitting meditation, and to extol the profound benefits of sitting meditation without setting it up in opposition to the rest of our active lives. Bottom line, as I understand it: there is just life!

Of course, each of you has a different temperament that needs to be honored. Some people naturally are drawn to do much more sitting, at home or in meditation centers. Others, perhaps more extroverted, will sit less but bring more attention to daily life and to other practices. Some will use the breath more, some less. The criterion is pragmatic: Does it help you let go and suffer less? Be kinder and more sensitive to others? If you are fully in the present moment, you are practicing, whether sitting in the bathroom or in a mountaintop hut. The present moment has immense significance. It's inexhaustible.

When people come for interviews, I often ask, "How's your practice going?" Usually I hear in return, "Well, I don't get to sit very much." Then I say, "No, I asked about your practice. I didn't ask, 'How is your sitting practice.'"

Fellow dharma students, please remember that what matters is the quality of your mind, not the number of hours you sit. Is the mind developing the skill of understanding and letting go? Are you learning to unlearn what is harmful without being aversive, and how to nourish what is beneficial without getting attached? Is there more relaxed, alert continuity to your mindfulness? Less harshness with yourself when you have been inattentive? Fall asleep . . . wake up . . . fall asleep . . . wake up. That's it.

Most likely, in every age and every culture, human beings have suffered from the tendency to lose focus and to become distracted from a chosen task or activity. But it seems especially pernicious in our present time. In a world of continual distraction, if you become bored for even a moment or two, you need a distraction from your distractions. It's a bit like watching CNN—which I often do, even though it can be another form of suffering. On that channel, as I'm watching the main news picture, in the upper right-hand corner an army general shows up talking and I watch him, too. If I become bored with him, there's a crawl below, which has nothing to do with either the general or what's on the main screen. Just as I'm getting interested in the crawl, it is cut off by a commercial. Then the cycle starts again.

Is it any wonder that we need an old Chinese cook and his eventual student, Dogen? We need them desperately.

The Japanese word *shikan* is a good one to remember at this point. You might recognize it from the term *shikantaza*, a form of sitting meditation similar to what some of you do in your vipassana practice; it means, "just sitting." It was then applied to "just cooking." The word "just" in this context means *exclusively*. It means giving our wholehearted attention. When you cook, just cook.

Dogen's "Instructions to the Cook" can help us ease the problem of constant distraction. The cook is instructed to take the same care of the pots, pans, and culinary ingredients as he would of his own eyes. This teaching tries to convey an attitude of deeply connecting with each activity you do: you give yourself over to it by bringing all your senses to bear on it. It could be cooking a meal. It could be weeding a garden. Listening to your partner. Hugging your child. It could be tying your shoelaces. There's nothing special about tying your shoelaces, but the way you perform even this simple act can show your respect for your own life, however it is expressed in a given moment.

Breath awareness is one method that can help you develop full attention to otherwise easily overlooked moments of daily life. Using this practice throughout the day transforms many small and simple activities into meaningful chances to develop a mind that is focused, calm, and alert. Perhaps you stop at a red light—for about ten or fifteen seconds, instead of turning on the radio, just feel the breath as you sit there. When you go into a restaurant, just before you start to eat, simply notice the food on your plate. Look at your sandwich, tune in to your breathing, and see that you can be aware of your breathing and the sandwich, as you pick it up and bring it to your mouth.

Feel the breath as you wait for an elevator. Sit in a public park and accompanied by mindful breathing attend to some aspect of nature. In a doctor's office, rather than pick up a magazine or send an e-mail, stay with the breath as you wait for your appointment. Remember, patience is a *parami*, one of the ten virtues in Buddhist teachings. Become a patient patient, using the breath to calm the anxiety of waiting or to directly see your own impatience.

Recently, I heard from a yogi who used the practice of breath awareness during a morning of potential jury duty. For several hours, she was ushered from room to room in a grim courthouse. In her mind, what stretched ahead was dullness, physical discomfort on old wooden seats, and cursory magazine reading. But the entire scenario changed when she realized that she had been presented with a perfect morning to practice. This transformed her experience. She remained calm and alert throughout the process, sitting in the courthouse, using the breath as an anchor. In the end, she was not chosen to serve on the jury. But while others around her struggled with restlessness and boredom, she gained a priceless insight.

In most situations, you can practice breath awareness with eyes opened or closed. I have been a "people watcher" (and bird watcher, too) since childhood, so for me, open eyes and conscious breathing are simultaneously in the service of wakefulness. Since I travel often by public transportation, I'm with my breathing when I sit on the bus or train, aware of my fellow passengers. This looking is relaxed, casual and open-ended, and tries to not create self-consciousness in others. It simply helps me notice the human environment with a bit more clarity, while at the same time enlivening and calming the inner landscape.

In the presence of nature or art, it is easier for the mind to quiet down and to rest in the present moment. Real beauty, whether a Monet landscape or the sounds of the ocean, possesses that power: it overwhelms thinking. But no matter where you find yourself, you have the ability to help the mind quiet down. Wherever you go, the breath is with you, providing an anchor. At moments that are right for you, you can turn to it just as you might turn to a good friend, to help you stay alert and cut down on the mind's habitual, unnecessary thinking that often squanders so much energy.

If this breathing technique is new for you, it may not feel comfortable at first. That's fine. Give it a try, see what happens, and learn from it. Try not to turn it into a grim and dreary "assignment." If you forget to breathe mindfully while you are doing the dishes, do not berate yourself and add more suffering to your life! At a certain point—and the point is different for each of you—the technique of breath awareness may dissolve itself and simply become a natural way of life that puts a premium on attention, sensitivity, and interest in learning from daily experiences as you live them out right to the end. What matters most is the quality of mind you bring to whatever you do.

. . . . .

Q: My long afternoon drive home always tires me. Often I play music to generate liveliness. But when I have an emotional reaction to the music, I want to remove that from my experience of just driving.

A: Why? Your reaction to the music is a valid part of your experience. There's nothing wrong with music, unless it is a compulsion, as it is for some people. When that happens, you will do anything to keep from just being with yourself: you switch to channel music, just as you might switch to channel *metta*, or to channel breath. Mindfulness teaches you about your motives. If you are just enjoying music, that's neither bad nor good. It's just one of the joys of life. It depends on how you relate to it—and of course, in your example, it depends on how it affects your driving!

. . . . .

Q: I'm one of those people who automatically turns on the radio and even speeds up the car to avoid the boredom of the same daily route between home and work. It's a pattern I've tried to break—and failed.

A: Let me tell you about a student who routinely arrived ten minutes late to every evening meditation practice group at our urban center. He entered the hall and raced to his cushion, huffing and puffing. Eventually, I learned that the distance he had to travel necessitated driving very quickly. Otherwise, he would miss even more minutes of the group.

When a predicament such as this one comes up in daily life, the question is, Can the car go rapidly but the mind remain at peace? In other words, how does the external speed rate affect the mind? I've been a passenger with an ex-racing car driver going at top speed and felt completely safe, and I've been with slow drivers who make me want to jump out of the car.

When you're bored with your driving route, here is one suggested practice: see the anguish. *Oh no, not that gas station again, not that same smiling school crossing guard.* Or watch the tension build at a stoplight or in a traffic jam. Of course, mainly focus on your driving. It's fine to listen to music, too. But now and then, listen to your own reactions. If you do, you might see these habitual reactions start to weaken and fall away, and fresh mindful responses arise. Don't attempt to be calm; be aware of the tension and boredom. This awareness can naturally lead to an authentic calm.

Using this approach, the late-arriving student eventually learned that even when he had to drive at the maximally safe speed limit, he could be at peace. The car sped up but the mind did not. It required time and patience to learn how to do this practice, which I consider a fine example of engaged stillness.

· · · · ·

Q: *Just a few weeks ago, I was unexpectedly laid off from a job I'd had for twelve years. Can meditation help me get through this period without backsliding to all my old, not-so-healthy coping strategies?*

A: More and more practitioners report being out of work, or facing a shortened workweek. It is a rare person who would not be overwhelmed by this type of loss, especially if supporting others in the family. Often, even experienced yogis feel their whole world crumbling beneath them and can't change recurrent feelings of helplessness.

Ultimately, though, a trained mind gives you a far better chance to move from catastrophe to solution. It helps you see options obscured by the anxious or confused mind. You're not as helpless because you know that everything is workable, whether you're on the cushion or in a downsized manufacturing plant. Even in a world of impermanence and change, you are learning how to live with wisdom. The Buddha says, "All I teach is suffering and the end of suffering." He is talking about the suffering located in the mind, which is added to inevitable physical decay, natural disasters, and other tragedies we humans face. This suffering emanates from the psyche. If you understand the difference, at least you can weaken what the Buddha calls "the second arrow"—the suffering that strikes the mind.

If you cannot distinguish between the nature of your mind-made suffering and the actual job loss, you have mental sorrow. Often, you have torment. If you can make this distinction, a terrible situation such as losing a job and income still exists—but it isn't hopeless. Can you see the benefits of facing a complicated situation with a clear mind, rather than one desperately groping for a solution?

. . . . .

Q: When you talk about how to cope with losses, it brings up an old confusion of mine about meditation and therapy. Can you help me differentiate between the two?

A: Your question is important because we live in the culture of psychotherapy. In recent years, many approaches integrate psychotherapy with meditative practice, and a growing number of experienced psychotherapists are now also committed meditators. When it's been appropriate, I have suggested that a number of yogis work with these psychotherapists while continuing to meditate, and the outcomes have been beneficial. I have also suggested that people drop meditation for awhile, if psychotherapy seems more appropriate.

Perhaps the hard and fast boundary between the two approaches is dissolving. But since I've never been in therapy, and am not trained in that profession, I'm not truly qualified to answer your good question.

· · · · ·

Q: *I am trying to integrate choiceless awareness with practice in daily life. It's so much more complicated than when I am on the cushion because life bombards me with choices and distractions.*

A: Let me answer by giving you a personal experience. One beautiful summer Sunday afternoon I was walking along the Charles River in Cambridge, Massachusetts. Awareness was panoramic, taking in the river, geese in flight, a clear blue sky, and picnickers on the grass. Suddenly, an overturned car came into view, with a person lying on the ground beside it. Automatically, the panoramic view became focused. The all-inclusive world I was joyfully inhabiting was reduced to that one tragic scene.

It was not necessary to calculate what to attend to. Zooming-in was the right response to the situation. As in all moments of choiceless awareness, life itself set the agenda.

Now let me generalize from that one dramatic incident to try to give you a broader guide to practice in daily life. I'll put it in the form of a question that has been of immense help to me and to countless yogis over the years: What is correct action right here and now? Often in life, the answer is totally clear, such as at the sight of a car accident. But even when it's clear, do you bring full awareness to it? Are you intimate with the action, or separate from it? Are you fully aware of the present moment or are you already imagining how you will tell your friends about what happened? Practice is a process of narrowing the gap between you and the doing.

If you have a child, you might hug him or her every day. OK, hug! But when you hug, is half your mind still at work? If it is, the seeing of nonattention can bring you more fully back to your child. This is correct action.

Your practice leads you out of fragmented contact with reality.

Driving? OK, drive! Texting on your iPhone? OK, text! Each time and place calls for a unique response. You are engaged in an ongoing form of learning. This is the beauty of the practice: potentially, everything you encounter in daily life is your teacher—and learning how to live, moment to moment, provides its own fulfillment.

· · · · ·

Q: I understand that meditation should not include striving for goals or accomplishments. But what will motivate me to continue the practice in daily life if I'm not looking to improve my marriage or my work situation?

A: It is only natural that you want to improve your marriage and work. Does vipassana meditation help you do this? Yes. But perhaps not in the way you might expect.

Different models of practice offer different approaches. The stepladder approach, as it is sometimes called, includes a series of stages: first stage of practice, second stage, and so forth, somewhat analogous to BA, MA, and PhD. For many yogis, this structured approach is useful because they learn best by striving to get to the next level. It can stir up productive energy for practice.

I lived that way myself for a number of years spent in university life. I was quite at home in it until I realized that my life was filled with conflict and anxiety as I strived to climb higher on the ladder of academic success. Personally, I've done enough of that method. But please understand that the model of teaching that I use does not advocate that you throw up your hands and become indolent and fatalistic. Rather, it's seeing practice and realization as the same experience. That's how the Japanese Zen master Dogen describes it.

How, then, do you get to where you want to go with your practice and your life? This is a daunting question. Sometimes, as you meditate, you become even more purposeful: "I'll do this mindfulness stuff but only if it gets me where the books promise I will go." The mind constantly tries to move from A to B. More ambitious minds desire to move from A to Z in one big leap. But the practice is learning how to get from A to A.

Don't put your faith in a "future you" who will evolve over a number of retreats and sittings. Of course, you will reap byproducts down the road. But you do not have to wait, because meditation is a never-ending process of learning how to skillfully relate to everything daily life presents. Confirmation and verification occur right here and now!

Actually, this seeming passivity actually sets in motion a dynamic energy that does move you in a wonderful direction. But don't divide your attention with a preoccupation to improve. In our approach, you're not attaining specific stages of wakefulness, or of life goals, but rather taking care of each moment, whether on the cushion or at home or in school. This is why you are encouraged to not separate practice and daily life.

The Buddha is considered a fully awakened human being. He is offering you help to join him. Each moment of awareness is a small moment of Buddha mind. As the wakefulness matures by applying it to every occurrence in life, off and on the cushion, you will see the by-products of the learning that comes from this enhanced awareness. You are learning how to live skillfully in every moment, whether on retreat or at home with your family, at work with colleagues, or with strangers on the bus.

5

Awareness in Relationships

. . . .

To live is to be in relationship.   —VIMALA THAKAR

Can we be with each other without the heavy influence of old images, even though we have collected images of ourselves and each other over a whole lifetime? Are we aware of how these images color and distort our perceptions of each other? How they actually prevent us from perceiving anything accurately this moment? If we clearly understand this, can we carefully—caringly—look again as though for the very first time? Is it possible to look at each other and listen to each other in an entirely new way—not habitually driven to correct or change each other according to our likes and dislikes? Can we newly discover what is actually going on this instant and respond from clarity rather than from ideas?   —TONI PACKER

YEARS AGO, I practiced in the Thai forest tradition. To me, a forest is a place where you go on a picnic or search for ferns and mushrooms. But what I found in Thailand was a jungle with snakes, insects, and twisted tree vines. I wouldn't want to go on a picnic where our little huts were located. I told my teacher that while he taught in the Thai "jungle" tradition, I practiced in the Cambridge jungle tradition.

He said, "Cambridge? That's a big city with universities, isn't it?"

I said, "Yes, but it has people. Your jungle is populated with snakes and wild animals. My jungle is populated with people!"

Can bringing the practice of awareness in relationships enrich your life? Of course! But that simply states the obvious. You spend most of your lives in relationships. I believe that right there, as you interact with friends, partners, children, colleagues, neighbors, and strangers, you have the potential to enter a powerful dharma practice. I am not describing a method to merely make life more comfortable and peaceful. I am suggesting that in the contemporary world, awareness in relationships is as legitimate and potentially liberating as more traditionally taught practices.

Of course, you do not drop awareness, with or without the support of breathing. You bring it into relationships.

Some of you may be reluctant to take on relationships as an authentic dharma practice. However, in my eyes, this is truly unfortunate because so much of our life is lived in the presence of others. I urge you to enter interpersonal living in the spirit of the *Kalama Sutta,* where, as you recall, the Buddha encourages you to investigate and ask questions. Can you remain aware of your conditioned reactivity to other people, especially your most intimate relations? Can you maintain equanimity or see its absence in the midst of human interactions? Can you learn to do this without judgment or reproach?

The breath is with you in every moment—though in this approach you do not always turn to it because of the often swift and intense pace of interpersonal dynamics. That's fine. I've noticed in my own interactions, and heard reports from many yogis, that breath awareness practice can even interfere with practice in relationship. This happens when you focus more on the breath than on what's happening between you and the other person. Or when you find that fear of losing touch with your breath makes you unable to keep up with the high speed of human exchanges. This is a misuse of breath awareness meditation.

It's up to each of you to discern when breath awareness is a useful method and when it is not. As the breath helps you develop a clearer mind, it also helps develop the wisdom to know when it is skillful to use breath awareness in relationships and when it is not. Please don't be surprised if most of your practice in relationships does not include breath awareness. Just as in the formal sitting, when you dropped the breath and practiced choiceless awareness, relationships will often move your practice in this direction.

With time and continuity, awareness in relationships reveals the process of self-ing—of making "I" the center of the universe. And because it teaches you again and again about the true nature of self, it has the potential to take you to the unconditioned, *suññatā*, emptiness, or engaged stillness.

Usually when yogis hear me talk about this approach, it makes immediate sense: you see that if your practice omits relationship, it will be fragmented and of limited value. You also see the potential of reaching harmony in your home, or office, or even within yourself. Still, the most well-intentioned student stumbles and often falls, again and again, as he or she begins shining the light of awareness on relationships. This approach needs gentle, relaxed patience and careful observation. Wasn't your mind confused when you began to practice the first step, just watching the mind while you breathe? Now you're practicing in the heat and fire of your most complex condition: relationships in daily life.

Please keep in mind that when I use the term *relationship*, it is not limited to intimate bonds. It includes all moments when you are in the presence of another person. It can even encompass your relationships with objects, nature, art, and ideas. Of course, first and foremost, it is your relationship to yourself. Looked at from this perspective, life *is* relationships. Even when you are sitting alone, you are learning about yourself by relating to what the mind produces and how the body behaves.

My understanding of relationship as a vehicle for self-discovery is derived from what I learned forty years ago from Krishnamurti. To him, relationship, awareness, and learning comprised an inseparable practice. Of course, he appreciated the preciousness and benefits of sitting in solitude. But he underscored the urgency of sensitivity and learning in relationship. This became crystal clear to me at the conclusion of the days that we spent together when he visited the campus where I taught many years ago. I asked, "Can you give me some homework, something I can do?" He responded: "Pay attention to how you *actually* live!"

I can't do justice to the way he spoke those words. He looked at me eye to eye; his voice had electricity in it. And he repeated the phrase: "How you *actually* live." Then he elaborated: Not how you think you should live. Not how religious teachings tell you to live. Not how your parents tell you how to live. But how you *actually* live.

That "assignment" pierced through me. It is where I began my practice. By nature, I am contemplative and I love extended solitary retreats. But I did not begin with the belief that sitting was the star of the show. I understood from the start that the entire spectrum of people in my life, from parents to the cashier in the local grocery store, was not outside my practice.

Since then, my own practice and my work with countless yogis have strengthened the conviction that the practice of relationship is urgent not only for practitioners, but for the world we inhabit. Is global peace possible without peace between human beings in relationship to one another?

At Cambridge Insight Meditation Center (CIMC), we are committed to the practice of awareness in relationship. But not everyone shares our belief that this is a genuine dharma practice—underline *dharma*. This hit home when a prominent vipassana teacher came to the center, asking for tips about starting his own new urban center. He and I fully agreed about beliefs and methods, until I explained our system of interviewing students. Unlike traditional centers, where teachers give formal interviews mainly on retreats, we offer them throughout the year. During these regularly scheduled meetings, which are quite a bit longer than the ones on retreats, we question people about their daily lives. Inevitably, the subject of relationships often dominates the talks.

The visiting teacher was puzzled by this approach. His questions made good sense: Wouldn't the usual ten-minute dharma interview be adequate to cover the real issues of practice? Why not recommend that yogis see a well-trained therapist if they want to talk at length about problems in daily life?

I had known from the start of CIMC that we would need to balance innovative approaches with the rich and ancient tradition of vipassana. Fortunately, I received wise advice about this from many teachers—some of them more likely than others. My close colleague and very dear friend Corrado Pensa introduced me to one of his teachers, a Carmelite nun, Sister Paula, and she profoundly influenced the future of CIMC. When I met her after I taught a retreat in Italy twenty-five years ago, she had lived for twenty-six years on the grounds of her totally contemplative sect, surrounded by a mesh fence. Without ever stepping outside that space, she trained seven resident nuns and countless visitors.

I spent a full week in the nunnery. Twice a day, I met with Sister Paula, a wonderful human being with a fresh and alert mind and a great sense of humor. When I spoke with her about my wish to emphasize the relationships that comprised a vast territory of lay students' lives, she asked, "Is there any accountability?"

Her response puzzled me, so I asked her to explain. "I've listened to you now for a week," she said, "and it sounds like people account for their sitting and retreat practices. You talk with them about these, which is a form of accountability. It also tells them that you genuinely value their formal meditation practice. But if you instruct students to bring mindfulness and discernment into their relationships and then never ask about it, they don't think it is a serious or meaningful part of the dharma life. You just encourage them to go out and do it, but offer no channel to share the outcomes of applying mindfulness in their relationships."

In other words, she told us that unless we asked pointed questions, we would not convey the message that awareness in relationships is a true dharma practice. On returning to Cambridge, we implemented her wise advice in two ways. First, in practice groups and interviews, the guiding teachers asked about relationships and daily life. We used the same time-tested dharma principles, framed by the four noble truths, and applied them to interpersonal situations.

The challenge for me is to listen to these issues not as a skillful psychotherapist, which of course I am not—but rather to listen with a dharma ear.

I also created a new retreat model, called the sandwich retreat. It runs for two weekends—the two slices of the bread of the sandwich—and every weekday evening in between, which are the fillers. On the weekends, formal sitting and walking are practiced, as in any vipassana retreat. Weekdays comprise mindfulness of the content of our daily life and the learning derived from this attention. On those evenings, as we talk it over together, using dharma principles, students are reporting to us—so once again, there is a system of accountability.

In Thailand, and in many tropical countries where there is frequent flooding, people's homes are often damaged or totally lost. This gave rise to the forest master Ajahn Chah's reflection: "If you lose your home because of a flood, is it possible to not lose your mind?"

Without doubt, tragic events happen in each of your lives. The subtler question is, "What is your reaction to it? What's your relationship to what happens?" Here, the Buddha's teaching is revolutionary and also simple. It's an attempt to change your relationship to your life experience, whatever that is, including your relationships to other human beings. Most of the time, you are either grasping or pushing away what's happening to you. These habitual reactions come from not understanding where particular actions lead in the present moment and beyond.

In my experience, nothing flushes out reactivity more dramatically than relationships, especially the most intimate ones. Your reactions are mechanical. It is the same as when you prick your finger with a pin: you bleed. In American culture, we say that someone "pushed my buttons." Your buttons get pushed and your reflexes swing into action because they are conditioned. They are old programs, perhaps slightly modified in the present, and they react automatically.

Mostly, you look, listen, and speak with yesterday's eyes, ears, and voice, often believing that reflexive, dramatic reactions are a sign of spontaneity. But should you take pride in this habitual way of doing things? It is possible to go through an entire life repeating these same negative patterns over and over, and only to some degree modify them. Relationships are fluid and dynamic, each moment spawning new conditions. Yet rather than respond to the other person in the new and present moment, you tend to impose on them fixed images from the past. All of us are especially prone to do this with our closest companions.

In a wonderful story from the Islamic Sufi tradition, the wise fool Mullah Nazrudin sits under a tree eating hot red peppers. As he eats them, tears flow from his eyes. Still, he picks up another one and then another. People around him finally ask, "Mullah, why are you eating these red-hot peppers?" He responds, "I keep waiting for a sweet one."

Is it possible to extinguish the red-hot fire of reactivity? I know you do not have to passively hope and pray that, next time, you will react with kindness and calm. I know you can dissolve conditioned patterns. How? You do this by bringing our old friend awareness, with or without the support of the breath, to the fact of your reactions.

As you work with this approach, you catch yourself in the very moment of your conditioned reaction of anger at a spouse, or disappointment in a child, or frustration with a parent. When the energy of this direct seeing touches the energy of reactivity, a new approach opens though self-understanding. Awareness transforms mechanical reactivity into a fresh and genuine responsiveness because it emerges from a clearer mind. You see the present moment accurately, rather than imposing fixed conclusions from the past. A reaction is old, stale; a response, fresh, appropriate.

I'd like to share an exchange with a yogi that represents many of the reports I hear from students. Please keep in mind that often the most seemingly mundane situation can yield the deepest understanding of the Buddha's teaching. This "simple" story concerns a husband in a loving, long-term marriage who could not understand his chronic irritation with his wife. Her style of speech often irked him, as did her frequently intense, passionate outbursts about her family and friends. Sometimes he became deeply enraged by her behavior, and despite years of formal meditation and practice in daily life, his reactions generated repetitive arguments and rough patches in their lives.

I suggested that the yogi focus on the approach of awareness in relationships. He began this practice, and though he moved away from Cambridge, recently I received a letter that described how he had reached a point where he no longer reacted with annoyance to his wife's behavior. Gone were the conditioned reactions of *I hate when she talks so loudly. She has to calm down!* Instead, when he felt impatience with her outbursts, he turned awareness inward, to his own state of irritability. By doing this again and again, over a long period of time, he realized that his recurrent impatience stemmed from his desire for his wife to behave according to his needs, not hers. Rather than falling into habitual modes of reactivity—*when my wife speaks in a certain tone, I react automatically with annoyance*—he broke the cycle by focusing awareness on what was happening in the moment, which included both her words and his reaction to them.

Self-discovery and awareness have this affect. First, when the yogi observed his annoyance at his wife, his reactivity diminished. Ultimately, it disappeared. Rather than see her through the scrim of his patterned reactions of impatience or anger, he viewed her with fresh eyes. At the same time, he assured me, he did not disengage or detach but remained mindful of both his wife and his own inner reactions. Right there, in his kitchen, staying in the moment, he used the practice of being present in relationships.

By doing this, he made the crucial shift from judgment to understanding. This is available to all of you. With practice, you learn to stay in touch with your inner reactions, and at the same time remain fully attentive to others. Sometimes your attention is more with the other, but you have not lost touch with yourself; sometimes it is the opposite, and you are far more aware of yourself than of others. It's like the tide moving in and out. I use this practice of moving attention back and forth when I interview dozens of yogis within a short period of time, and so I know from my experience that it is an approach that helps keep the mind fresh and open to each new encounter.

At the end of the yogi's thoughtful and generous letter, he told me that his marriage was now far more satisfying. He had loved his wife throughout the years of their ups and downs. Now that he had used his practice to break the cycle of proliferated irritation, his most intimate relationship was harmonious. No small feat.

The ancient Chinese used the image of the host to describe the observing, stable meditator. Many guests visit the host. Some are invited, and they tend to be kind, charming, and a pleasure to entertain. Others are not invited: they are drunk, unruly, and eat all the food. Or they stand around, staring into space.

If you become so absorbed in the behaviors of your guests that you forget you're in charge, you are no longer the host. Can you stay awake in the face of all the diverse visitors who come and go? This is your practice when you sit. To be the host. To be awareness itself.

Is it more challenging to be the steady, calm host when you practice with relationships? Of course! At times you are so overwhelmed by sensations and emotions, you are "blinded" and cannot even see the other person or group of people in front of you. You're lost in your confusion, or joy, or desire. The image of the host is intended to remind you to remain fully attentive to the other person, and to hear and see what they say and do in the present moment. At the same time, it reminds you to keep in touch with yourself. Here again is the ebb and flow of attention.

As you develop this practice, the filter of past images dissolves itself through the seeing-energy of awareness. Perhaps you and your teenage child have repeated the same exchange, in one form or another, hundreds of times: you yell at her to clean her room and she slams the door, shouting, "Leave me alone!" You shout back, or withdraw in angry silence. She refuses to come to dinner. On and on it goes. In Buddhist teachings, the word *papanca* is used to describe this cascade of reactions. Emotions proliferate, and deep suffering ensues.

When you respond with the clear, fresh mind of awareness, you weaken *papancas* and break the cycle of reactivity. Even if you repeat the same words as before, their impact is altered. You might say, "Please put away those clothes and books and stuffed animals." If your mind is fresh and your energy benign, there is a better chance that your child listens and responds in kind. But if those same words emerge from reactivity, they are fueled by anger. When that happens, the other person can't hear you, because they feel attacked. In many situations, we humans are defending ourselves against these real or anticipated attacks. Sometimes we know it; often we do not.

Relationships and learning work in tandem. In a sense, the practice of relationship is a lifelong continuing education course. To me, such lifelong learning is the juice of this approach. I promise that if you keep coming back to it, you will find an inexhaustible source of material to help you move from judgment to understanding and from conditioned reactions to fresh, authentic responses.

As this happens, the mind that sees the other person expresses itself through wiser and kinder actions. This is not a response that you can grasp or control. It emerges from a mind that is quiet and clear.

Many yogis willing to take on relationships as a genuine practice are satisfied when they reach a peaceful, comfortable relationship with their partner, children, or coworkers. This is an invaluable development along the path of both psychological and spiritual growth. Yet if you are willing to use awareness of relationship to go beyond this point, the next step can bring you even further on the inner journey; it can bring you to a deep understanding of the true nature of the original mind, unclouded by accumulated conditions.

Relationships, especially your most intimate ones, relentlessly push the self-ing button. It's where you encounter the greatest threats to fixed self-images and self-cherishing habits.

In a number of suttas, the Buddha teaches that the root of suffering is the attachment to me and mine. When you investigate deeply the four noble truths, which teach that suffering is caused by craving and attachment, you see that it is *me* who desires and resists letting go. Dharma practice is about freedom from suffering by forgetting or going beyond the self. Our old friend Dogen, the Japanese Zen master, put it beautifully: "To study Buddhadharma is to study the self. To study the self is to forget the self. To forget the self is to be awakened by all things." As he describes, the mind is no longer selfing. It's not preoccupied with itself. It's just present, awake, clear. In this way, you unearth the deepest problem you have, which is *you*. From my point of view, the most problematic person on this planet is Larry Rosenberg.

For the most part, what we call *me* is made up of our own story: where I was born, all that has happened since then, our familiar apprehensions, anxieties, yearnings, losses, and joys. There isn't a person reading this book who doesn't have a story. When you meet a new person, perhaps you unveil some of that. As your ties deepen, perhaps you revise the material. Sometimes you conclude that you're a model partner, friend, or employee. At other times, you feel hopeless about yourself in relationship to others. In nearly every encounter, you see tendencies well up and contradictions abound, and they all concern this dynamic bundle of energy that you've come to think of as being *me*.

But as the approach of awareness in relationships deepens, the notion of self changes. As you continue to watch your mind, you see nonstop mind-created images and fabrications. You understand that the story of *me* and *my life* is impermanent and insubstantial. All Buddhist traditions refer to this insubstantiality, or emptiness (*suññatā*) as the crown jewel of the Dharma. Empty of what? Empty of attachment to me or mine.

Do you want to let go of your story? Probably not—you have worked too hard at it. Look at all the time, energy, and money you've put into making up your self, and how you've cleansed it, exercised it, dressed it, and taken lessons to enhance it. You've gone to school and traveled to refine and improve it. Often, you're enthusiasts of making a bigger, better self. Perhaps you are stuck on self-improvement: a more spiritual self, even a more compassionate self.

Whatever it is, you're fixing up the personality, trying to make it better, polish it a little, or sandpaper it down.

With attentive practice, the time comes when the seeing is so clear and steady, it becomes much easier to let go of your story. What would the point be of holding on? Holding on to what? You grab and it's already gone, because your mood shifts or the conditions of your life alter. It's old news. Or what you believe yourself to be in one moment, or in one year, is contradicted by the changes life presents you. All the images and ideas that arise in the mind and present themselves as being *me*, which you normally identify with, actually start to become less interesting than what is in back of all those notions.

Put another way, self-knowing is discovering, in a profound way, everything that you are *not*. Mindfulness in relationships is a powerful way to flush out these misperceptions and to let go of attachment to My Story. The mathematics of this approach to dharma practice emphasize subtraction, not addition.

Does some self-improvement come along with practicing meditation? And increased self-esteem? Of course. But what I'm emphasizing here is that practice takes you in a far less conventional direction: it leads to liberation from the belief in a fixed and stable entity called *self.* You start to see thoughts—"I'm a wonderful person" or "I'm a jerk"—as merely thoughts. You abandon the safety of fixed notions, such as "I'm infallibly calm in a crisis" or "Without me, this organization would fall apart." You see that if cherished self-images are concocted by habits of the conditioned mind, then your only true security is in the mind that is clear and free of conditioning from the past: free of cultural and personal stories.

All methods and approaches of vipassana practice incline us from the conditioned to this unconditioned mind, pure awareness in and of itself. In other words, they free us from suffering.

A cartoon I came across while practicing Zen in Japan beautifully illustrates this understanding. Picture a Japanese Zen monk carrying a huge sack on his back. He is walking along a beach, barefooted, and bent over, with an expression of misery on his face. His tracks in the sand are deep as trenches. On the sack is the word *Me*.

. . . . .

In chapter 3, the section on choiceless awareness, we talked about the power and beauty of the silent mind that can arise in formal meditation. Now we're bringing that quality into the realm of everyday relationships. Please remember that this silence is limitless. It reaches far beyond your encounters with your families and closest friends. It extends to colleagues, employers, and bus drivers. It becomes a way of living that ripples farther and farther out.

But first, a word of caution about the nature of the silent mind. Sometimes when you read Buddhist texts, it sounds as if the silent mind infallibly acts with wisdom and compassion. But no matter how clear your seeing-energy becomes, no matter how wise and compassionate you believe yourself to be with people in your lives, every moment needs attention. The law of karma, of cause and effect, unceasingly operates in human encounters. What may appear wise and skillful in one exchange may turn out to be incorrect, or even harmful. And you cannot predict the effect of your words or actions on other people. Watch and learn!

In other words, even when you respond from the highest wisdom manifesting at the time, mistakes will be made. This is true in your personal relationships, and also even when you are relating to nature, money, food, sex, or sports.

Of course you take full responsibility for your actions. But as meditators, you also learn that a seemingly bad situation can actually be a good situation. Why? Because it gives the opportunity to learn about yourself and to become free of old patterns. Put another way, mistakes can help move your mind from its conditioned to unconditioned state. They can be the occasions for wisdom.

Thich Nhat Hanh likens our experiences to compost, and I think that image is apt. Most people look at patterns of reactivity as garbage to be tossed away; dharma practice turns them into fuel that grows nourishing, organic food. You grow wiser by learning from the mistakes you make and seeing your foolishness and lack of wisdom. By the same token, if you avoid looking directly at your mistakes and learning from them, you also avoid wising up.

Remember the Buddha's teaching in the *Kalama Sutta:* wisdom is not fixed. It is alive, and it is tested and learned from moment to moment. You will make mistakes in your actions. You will do foolish things. You will hurt people. Some of you will learn from the rich vein of mistakes, and others, unfortunately, will not. If you do learn, then the practice of meditation can become an endlessly interesting journey rather than an abstract goal.

The pilgrimage is inside, in our minds and hearts. That's where the real journey takes place. The breath can help us make this inner journey. It is the place where many meditators begin. Some of you will continue to use the breath as a vehicle as you catch more and more glimpses of the unconditioned mind. Others will choose among the many other methods that the Buddha left for us, including the method of no method, or choiceless awareness.

This book devotes special attention to daily life and relationships because these are often avoided, neglected, or deemed less spiritual than "official" formal practice. But please remember, as I've said before: Life is prior to *all* methods, whether it is life in the form of sitting on a cushion or in the form of washing the dishes. Craving and aversion can arise everywhere. Each element of life makes the choice of correct action clear, in a given moment. Wherever you are, awareness and breath are methods to help you stay awake, learn, and become free in every aspect of life. They are designed to help you live skillfully so your life is beneficial to you and to others. Isn't that why you practice meditation, whether on retreats or in daily life?

The Buddha presented us with one person's view of living. He was a human being who attempted to explore the depths of the human psyche, find out what his suffering was about, and share some of that with us. For me, he is a guide to living, and fortunately, like you, I've been invited to investigate the teachings. As I continue to see confirmation of his teachings in my own life and the lives of others, more energy and joy has arisen. So I continue to practice.

But if it were proven that the Buddha never existed—that a bunch of brilliant people at a great university think tank dreamed him up and put together teachings that they claimed to be almost three thousand years old, then translated into Pali and Sanskrit—you know what? I'd still keep doing it. Even if the linguistic and scholarly superstructure and historical accretions fell away and the teachings turned out to be manufactured, I'd continue to practice. Why? Because I haven't found a better way to live. Are *not* paying attention, *not* wanting to learn, and living in the wounds of the past, a better option? Of course not. Awareness and self-knowing are synonyms for being fully alive.

I'm grateful to someone called the Buddha, and for people who have kept the teachings alive for thousands of years. I was fortunate enough to receive them from extremely gifted teachers, and they have helped me tremendously. I hope they help you. But essentially, my job is to point you back to yourself. While there are suttas and techniques and approaches, and while you can all encourage and sometimes even inspire one another, finally, the challenging and joyful work is up to you.

No matter what degree of awakening you attain, to some extent you are in the lineage of the Buddha. You enter that stream by taking care of the present moment—where practice and awakening, where the unconditioned and awareness, are the very same things. As you practice, you open to deeper degrees of truth about yourself, others, and the nature of the mind. More and more, you live in awareness.

As we conclude this reflective guide to practice, I would like to share with you my first and probably last poem. If there is some vanity in this, forgive me: no doubt it has to do with a lifetime bereft of poetic skill.

Some months ago during a peaceful and silent period of sitting meditation, "out of nowhere" came the brief intimations that follow. They came as a complete surprise, especially when I realized that the words were a highly condensed record of forty years of contemplative practice. I will leave them to you to unpack. I rejoice if it helps your own journey to freedom.

> Where is peace to be found?
> In the same place as sorrow.
> How convenient!

· · · · ·

Q: *You suggested that we listen to you with full attention, but my mind is filled with comments and judgments. Can you describe the practice of "just listening" to another person or to a group of people?*

A: The practice remains the same: be aware of what's actually happening. Just now, as you were speaking, my mind could begin to say, "Oh, this will be a long answer," or "I'm tired, I want to take a shower." Or I could mentally rehearse a fascinating remark that would bowl over everyone in the meditation hall.

But like you, I've taken on this practice. It encourages you to listen to the speaker and, simultaneously, listen to yourself. You will see the mind at work and learn that you listen to one another through a filter. It could be the filter of the past or the future. It could be the filter of anxiety or the desire to please.

This approach is not to force yourself to listen with your veins popping out of your neck. That would be exhausting! Rather, you're encouraged to be more open, sensitive, and alert. If you enlist the help of mindful breathing, which is always available, that's fine. As you listen, just begin to hear the trips taken by the mind—and learn from that. As your skill and sensitivity develop, the filter loses its force. Clarity of mind grows. The listening becomes free of grasping or aversion: it is just listening.

Here's an example from my own life that shows the nuances of skills in listening while actively involved in relationships. Often when my wife comes home, she shares her experiences of working at the hospital with troubled patients. Initially, this pushed a reactive button in me that produced a nice but unwanted dharma talk. In other words, I assumed she was asking me to solve the problem. In time, I realized that sometimes she did want an advisory opinion, but sometimes she simply wanted me to listen. This has been extremely beneficial in our exchanges together. My mind became more in touch with the emotional field from which the words emerged.

Refining the art of listening helps you move from reactivity to responsiveness. To develop this skill, some of you might find it helpful to situate yourself in nature and as you sit and breathe, listen to the sounds and the silence around you. Of course, this is always a wonderful way to spend time. Perhaps it could help you transition to the skill of listening in more highly charged environments with other people.

Skillful listening is underrated. Instead, enormous attention and respect is given to the art of speaking. Articulate, fluent talkers impress everyone—but the silent art of listening is equally creative and beneficial.

* * * * *

Q: Judging other people is a real problem for me. I see myself constantly judging, opposing, and resisting when I'm at work or even with friends. Then I judge myself for being judgmental. It seems like an endless cycle.

A: You're right. The judging mind creates an infinite regress. But just seeing that pattern is a large part of your practice. Look, some of our minds do not know how to react to anything in life except to judge: You're no good at this; you never were and never will be. But when you get caught up in the judging mind, or you strive to get rid of it, it only becomes stronger. You have to give it attention—even love. "Oh, here comes the judging mind. Poor thing. That's all it knows how to do." Regard it as if it were a difficult child: without attention and care, complicated problems might develop.

* * * * *

Q: Last week, I spent an evening with my eighty-eight-year-old mother. As I became caught up in her suffering and anxiety, and also judged it, I noticed what was happening. Then I moved past those states of mind.

A: Please remember that emotions will always pass. Even if you do not meditate, everything changes and shifts—but often an emotion remains "hot" as it moves along. In dharma language, the critical question to ask is whether the emotions go out hot or cold. In the light of awareness, emotions go out "cold." Like a defanged snake, a noise is made but the bite is not poisonous.

However, this is not at the expense of your ability to care for your elderly mother. An awareness practice is not a form of detachment; it is nonattachment. Intimacy and awareness coexist. In fact, the quality of nonattachment can liberate greater expressions of affection and love.

· · · · ·

Q: *Can you help me distinguish between a healthy attachment to my aging father, who is sick and suffering, and an unhealthy one?*

A: I hear this inquiry from many sensitive and caring yogis. Let me respond with a seemingly silly scenario that might illustrate a far more serious approach. It involves the mediation cushion that I sit on. I love it, I really do. It's the perfect seat. My knees and lower back do not hurt. It helps maintain an alert, upright posture. Unfortunately, though, it is not mine. It belongs to the meditation center.

Now, when it's time to leave the hall, what if I take the cushion home with me? What if the time comes to shower, and I'm so fond of my cushion that I go in with it? Then I come out and my wife says, "What are you doing with that soaking wet cushion? It's time for dinner." I say, "I'm coming to dinner but I must have my cushion with me."

If a little boy clutched this tightly to a teddy bear, he would be cute and lovable. But when you're eighty years old and walking around with a dripping wet cushion, you're in trouble.

In other words, life tells you when it's not a skillful attachment. How? By seeing that you begin to suffer. Remember, the Buddha tells us that everything that arises passes away. If you become fixated on anyone or anything in a changing world, how can that yield happiness? Life teaches us that awareness must be supple and flexible in response to changing conditions. Can you cherish a relationship or even an object that brings you joy, and then allow it to pass away? That's nonattachment. It's not an absence of love or even pleasure. It is non-clinging to love or pleasure.

However, this is your father! Wouldn't it be strange if you had no attachment? As your practice matures, you see the difference between love and holding on. Awareness weakens the attachment and also the self-pity, if it exists, but it does not weaken love. I know some of you believe that experienced meditators don't express strong emotions, or perhaps that they don't cry. Please don't set up an ideal of what it means to be the perfect yogi. You are all human—watch and learn!

*   *   *   *   *

Q: *Not too long ago, a lifelong friend ended our relationship. Though I've meditated for years, I'm not able to deal with the depth of sadness and confusion this brings up in me.*

A: I think everyone can empathize with this loss. It raises the same depth of suffering as other profound life changes we've talked about, such as the loss of parents or of jobs and income. So let me repeat, briefly, that as you equip the mind to be more steady and clear, everything can become workable because it is observable. You will find that this trained mind more easily grasps the lawfulness of change on both a macro- and microscopic level. The art of seeing includes understanding the impermanence of even the most seemingly fixed elements in your lives, such as your long-term relationships, homes, and once-steady employment. Are you willing to actively engage with the countless features of life that everyone inevitably loses, including even your youth, health, and life itself?

But I know that when you suffer a tremendous loss, such as the friendship you described, often you're too full of grief or anger to listen to these words. Even if you're a longtime yogi, the practice of vipassana meditation might seem out of reach. So I remind you once again that you can temporarily return to the breath as an exclusive object of attention. Or you can practice the second contemplation, using the breath as an anchor, to accompany you as you examine your suffering. If the time comes when the mind is more calm and stable, you can then directly observe the feelings of sorrow and loss.

. . . . .

Q: I'd like to return to the problem of practicing nonattachment in our most intimate relationships. What about those of us with children to raise and take care of?

A: This might be the most challenging one: mother and child. Mothers ask, "How can I not be attached to my child? I love my child." I say, "That's wonderful. Your child is fortunate." But then I encourage them to pay careful attention to see the distinction between love and attachment. I suggest that by using the practice of relationship, they may begin to notice the times when they grab hold and love, and the times when the grasping and holding on begins to weaken.

Awareness can soften many of the emotions that cause you to cling to the people you love most dearly. Let's take the example of anxiety. Last week, my granddaughter had a cold and fever. My wife, the grandma, became upset when the fever rose up, and happy when it lowered. Life at home was like the stock market. I told her that awareness could weaken her extreme reactions, and she said, "I don't know, should we take her to the emergency room?" Eventually, she agreed that paying attention to her own anxiety might weaken it. I urged her to try to take one day at a time, or one hour at a time.

Since she's not a meditator, I did not suggest that she take it moment by moment, but I do suggest that approach to those parents and grandparents who are yogis. If your mind remains steady and calm in the present moment, I promise you will not fail to respond to the medical or psychological crises that arise. Mindfulness does not make you a bad caregiver. Many of you might believe in a correlation between deep and extensive suffering and deep and extensive love.

But please remember that in the Buddha's teachings, suffering most likely indicates unskillful thoughts or behavior. It is not necessarily the best indicator of love.

As you deepen your practice of relationships, see if you respond more skillfully to your child's behavior, even at its most outrageous. See if your conditioned reactivity, which might be anxiety or anger or denial, weakens. Then observe whether your suffering diminishes—but not your love.

Again, don't set up the ideal of perfection! You are not monks or nuns—and even monastics are human, with deep emotions and attachments. The thrust of your practice is training in awareness and honesty, not hankering after an ideal. The drive to be perfect deflects much-needed energy away from attending to the truth of the present moment.

·   ·   ·   ·   ·

Q: Do you really believe that the practice of relationships in daily life can awaken us to the same degree as the formal practice of samadhi and vipassana? I hear you say these words, but I'm not convinced.

A: I appreciate your honesty. Deep down, many yogis do not believe that the dharma practice of relationships in daily life holds the same liberating potential as sitting and walking. Even when you hear a dharma teacher extol the meditative benefits of life off the cushion and you nod in agreement, most of you rank formal practice as superior.

Let me begin to answer this urgent question by asking you to pause for a few moments and to look into the question itself: Why do you doubt the value of relationship as an essential part of dharma practice? Bring awareness to the soil from which the question emerged. See what happens. Is there a feeling such as resistance or indifference? Please take this question home with you. Listen in silence.

Suffering is the time-honored condition that brings most people to Buddhadharma. Some enter monastic life—but most of you who are committed to meditative living do not wish to be monks or nuns. What to do? Spend maximum hours at meditation and retreat centers; nurture a sitting meditation practice at home; live an ethical life? Certainly! Even so, most of the day remains filled with other concerns and activities. You marry, work full-time, care for parents, pay credit card debts, and shop for organic food.

You need a practice appropriate to the realities of your life—to all of the realities, whether sitting in the hall or hugging your child at home. It is all one life: life in the form of sitting, life in the form of hugging. Is it at all necessary to compare and rank life's endless forms?

The Buddha's educational model is to hear dharma information, make sure you understand it, then test conceptual knowledge to find out whether it is skillful or not. In this sense, each teaching—including the value of relationships in daily life—is a working hypothesis to be investigated in the fire of actual living.

Have you done this? Your question suggests you may not have. This is not a criminal offense. However, start where you are, not where you think you should be. As soon as you're aware of doubt, you're back on the dharma path. You can doubt and resist any aspect of the teaching—even breath awareness. At the same time, remember the second method, breath-as-anchor, which teaches that you can use the breath to help you maintain samadhi as you insightfully awaken to the stresses in human interaction. Each of the three methods can help you observe every aspect of the way you actually live your lives, including your relationships.

Finally, let me repeat my belief that awareness in relationships is fertile ground for waking up. I will go out on a limb and say—as others have said—that relationship might be the richest source of revealing the power of attachment to me and mine, or self-ing. Remember, the Buddha identified self-ing as the root cause of sorrow.

Could it be that our encounters with partners, colleagues, and strangers hold the same potential to liberate us as sitting in a solitary room, mindful of breath? I encourage you all to investigate this possibility. As you do, it might help to remember the simple and beautiful words of the Chan master Sheng Yen: "Practice should not be separated from living, and living at all times should be one's practice."

Meeting Krishnamurti

INTRODUCTION

Why append my memories of Jiddu Krishnamurti to a book devoted to Buddhist meditation? Krishnamurti (K) was not merely critical of organized religion; he believed it was often an obstacle to self-discovery and a source of tremendous human suffering.

This emphatically nonsectarian man was my first teacher of dharma. When we met forty-five years ago, I was deeply confused about my life's work as a college professor, and his teachings helped me move toward what happily turned out to be my life's work: the study, practice, and teaching of meditation. In a sense, he is my last teacher, too. Over all these years, his unwavering insistence on direct seeing of our inner and outer life, and on learning from what we see, has invigorated and inspired my life.

I started with his teaching of choiceless awareness. Then why did I take up Buddhadharma for all these years? My answer is simple. As I mentioned in the introduction to this book, I realized I needed help. I needed years of Buddhist teachings and practice to put K's verbal teachings into authentic action. I needed the help of techniques, forms, special settings, community support, long periods of silent meditation alone and in groups. Above all, I needed other wonderful teachers who agreed that I needed guidance, and generously and patiently offered it. Especially, I was drawn to the Buddha's teaching on mindful breathing as a vehicle for developing calmness and insight.

Throughout these years of Buddhadharma, my contact and devotion to K and his teaching never wavered. He is my root teacher. Even from the grave, he continues to enliven my love of the Buddha's teaching. For these many decades, it has been a happy partnership.

I am in the good company of many Buddhist teachers who see the affinity between these two approaches. Put in the words of Ajahn Sumedho, a contemporary American vipassana master in the Ajahn Chah lineage: "With awareness, we can embrace the whole of it— the good, the bad, the right, the wrong, pleasure and pain—they all belong. It isn't a matter of trying to control the mind; it is more like 'choiceless awareness' in Krishnamurti's words. There is awareness and we don't choose anything; we don't try to hold onto this or get rid of that."*

Samdhong Rinpoche, a revered Tibetan lama close to the Dalai Lama, spent extensive time with K and concluded that no fundamental differences exist except that the Buddha taught from both the relative and absolute truth, and K from the absolute (in vipassana circles, this is referred to as the Unconditioned). The Dalai Lama himself held three private meetings with K. Dr. A. T. Ariyaratne, the world-famous engaged Buddhist often called the "Gandhi of Sri Lanka," told me that though he was born a Buddhist, he did not fully grasp what the Buddha had in mind in the *Satipathanna Sutta* until he heard K's clear and profound exposition of meditation. This list could go on.

K's influence suffuses the teachings in this book. The exploration in chapter 1 of the *Kalama Sutta* is a tribute to K's unrelenting emphasis on the qualities of investigation, doubt, learning, and also on testing the truth of the teachings in your own experience. All Buddhist teachers extol the spirit of inquiry, but over time, most of us settle into comfortable assumptions about our chosen teaching

---

* Ajahn Sumedho, *Don't Take Your Life Personally* (Totnes, UK: Buddhist Publishing Group, 2010), p. 281.

and practice. K did not. His teachings consistently rekindle the flame of inquiry, keeping us honest and open to what is happening here and now. The origins of this book go back to this teaching, which led me to question and reexamine whether my passion for choiceless awareness aligned with the reality of my students' skills and inclinations. When I realized it did not, I returned to more energized teaching on breath awareness.

Another strand of K's influence woven through these pages is the primacy of relationship as a practice. Again, this is a subject most Buddhist schools talk about, whether referring to the significance of relationships in monastic or lay life. Frequently, however, Buddhist teachings wisely rely on refuge in the precepts to guide harmonious living together. In K's hands, the substance of the precepts is present but the teachings expand to include relationship as a mirror to help you see self-ing. In the direct seeing of your relationship to life in all its forms, you weaken and even eliminate what the Buddha calls the source of suffering: attachment to me and mine. In other words, K converts the most problematic element of living into a practice in the service of liberation from sorrow. This understanding of relationship as practice is most fully investigated in the last chapter of this book.

Finally, K's influence is unmistakable in this book's emphasis on the inseparability of life and practice. Once again, I'm naming an approach sincerely taught in most Buddhist circles—and one that I've explored in the teachings of Dogen in the chapter on daily life. But long before I knew about Buddhism, K instilled in me this understanding. When he taught, he moved seamlessly from discourses on nature, to people in the city street, to material objects, to dynamics in the inner world. It was choiceless awareness in action. What is called *practice* and what is called *life* are identical: there is only life in its many forms!

At the end of my first meeting with Krishnamurti, he emphasized, "Pay attention to how you *actually* live"—not how you think you live, not how you think you should live! From that day on, this teaching was seared in me. To this day, it inspires my life, whether teaching, practicing, relating, walking—or writing the words in this book.

AN INTERVIEW, AUGUST 24, 2009

Madeline Drexler

· · · · ·

Q: Let's talk about the influence of Krishnamurti on your life and on your teaching.

A: To begin with, although he died in 1986, he is still very much alive in me. He's in my bones. Of all the teachers that I've had, he had the most powerful effect—far and away.

· · · · ·

Q: Because of what he was teaching or how he was teaching?

A: I can't make a separation—it was both. Who he was, and the content of his teachings, were like music to my ears. Some background information might be helpful. I met him in the late sixties—sixty-seven, sixty-eight. I was teaching social psychology at Brandeis University at the time. My colleague, Professor Morrie Schwartz—the key figure in the book *Tuesdays with Morrie*—started insisting that I meet K. He said, "Larry, I was in New York for the last few weeks, and I heard this Indian gentleman at the New School for Social Research. I didn't understand a word he was saying, but I know it's exactly what you're looking for. And he's coming to Brandeis."

I said, "Morrie, it's OK, it's OK." I wasn't drawn to what Morrie was telling me in the least. He said, "No, no, no, you really have to listen to him. It's what you've been looking for." I said, "Well, what was he talking about?" He answered, "I haven't got a clue. But I know it's for you. I really do."

I said, "OK, what's his name?" "J. Krishnamurti." I said, "Why is he going to be on the Brandeis campus?" He said that Professor James Klee, in the psychology department, had arranged it. Every year, they had a distinguished person come to Brandeis as a guest of the film department. Krishnamurti was invited to be in residence for a few days; his talks were to be filmed. I had never heard of him but decided to at least turn up and hear what he had to say.

I was in Harvard Square about a week before K was due to arrive, browsing at a highly intellectual, academic bookstore. I asked the owner if he had any books by someone called Krishnamurti. I was fairly confident that he would not be included in this gathering of profound thinkers. To my surprise, he directed me to the one book of K's on the shelf—*Think on These Things.*

I started leafing through it. How could such a book make its way into this bookstore? Krishnamurti was speaking to children about the challenges they faced growing up and meeting life. His language was simple, ordinary, concrete, and direct. I had never read anything that responded with such simplicity and depth to the fundamental challenges facing us all—ostensibly for children, while at the same time going straight to my heart, an educated professor in his mid-thirties. I was very moved. Any hesitation about attending his week of teaching was gone.

So Krishnamurti shows up. Now, one more contextual factor, which was a significant part of why this had such a powerful impact on me. At the time, a feeling of separation from academic life was emerging in me. I had been in the department of psychiatry at Harvard Medical School, which I mistakenly blamed for this problem. I left after only two years, returning to teach at the University of Chicago, where I had spent many happy years as a student. However, it turned out that it wasn't what I wanted, either, so I left after a year to accept an offer from Brandeis University.

What I learned at Harvard was very painful. I was all "puffed up" about teaching social psychology and doing research at Harvard. The honeymoon lasted about six months. I started to meet real people and see it's just life, just human beings full of vanity and neurosis and, often, unfulfillment. All my hopes were dashed.

For the first time in my life, I had money—for me. Women were much more interested in me now. I often wore a Harvard sweatshirt, had Harvard stationary, and was in many ways quite pleased with myself. I had my own apartment very close to Harvard Square, rather than always needing roommates, as in graduate school, in order to pay the rent. It was one version of the American dream, intensified by very proud family appreciation of such accomplishments. My father was a taxi cab driver from Russia with a fourth-grade education, and here I am in academic paradise!

But as time unfolded, I saw that I was still conflict-ridden and under self-imposed pressure to prove myself—to myself. There was a really outstanding resume. A book and many research articles had already been published while still a graduate student, mainly due to immense drive and hard work.

Then a certain disillusionment set in, as I mentioned—first finding fault with Harvard, then Chicago, and finally with Brandeis. Gradually I realized that there was nothing wrong with these great centers of academic learning. The problem was me! I was looking in the wrong place for the kind of inner peace and happiness that I so longed for. I had to start looking at myself. How do you do that? To begin with, squandering so much psychic energy blaming "the university" for failing to fulfill my deluded thinking started to drop away. There was a period of grief and sadness at the loss of what was, at one time, such a wonderful source of identity and security.

I hope that these few biographical remembrances can, to some degree, help the reader grasp why the meeting with Krishnamurti had such an immense impact on me. I was one very ripe banana!

· · · · ·

Q: This disillusionment is what Morrie Schwartz was alluding to?

A: Probably. I was always groping after New Age things and asking about psychedelic drugs, meditation, yoga, and diet. It was very early in my search—just scratching around. I really didn't know much.

When Krishnamurti arrived, there was already a decline in the passion I once had for academic study. I had been extremely enthusiastic about being a professor. I was really on fire about study, research, and the teaching of academic social psychology. But for a few embers, the flame had all but gone out. I knew so much *about* the mind—mostly other people's. What about my own?

So in comes Krishnamurti. The first day was informal. I was in a room with him. Morrie Schwartz set it up so that I could meet with him. Krishnaji—as he was called—and I sat down and began to chat. He was dressed beautifully: a British gentleman. As an aside, I recall smiling to myself and thinking that this is what the two Jewish senior professors must have meant with their advice to me as a young, nervous and new teacher at Harvard: "The secret of success here is to think Yiddish but dress British."

K wore exquisite clothing and shoes. His manner was courtly, warm and very friendly. But early in our conversation, I started to feel extremely uncomfortable. Why? We were just sitting there, and he had no agenda, seemed relaxed and at ease. Was it because he was world famous? No. Krishnaji was making fun of himself, being invited to come to a university to be the Man of the Year for this filming. With a full laugh, he said he had not read much and had never even been to college. After an hour or so we parted. I realized that I was so uncomfortable because he was extraordinarily attentive to me, yet at the same time quite relaxed.

Now I had already known people who were very attentive to me—for example, my mother and father. But there was tension in it : "What is this lunatic up to now? Up to no good in school again?" It was a loving, caring interest, but also tense and worried. I wasn't used to that quality of attention without tension. This was new to me. The first of many valuable lessons to be learned from Mr. J. Krishnamurti.

· · · · ·

Q: *How was his attentiveness conveyed? Did he sit forward and look at you?*

A: No, no, that's the whole point. It was all quite natural.

. . . . .

Q: He met your gaze? He asked you questions?

A: Yes, but mainly he was completely relaxed and appeared to be listening fully. It was not like, "Now I'm going to be attentive because here is a person coming in for an interview" or anything like that. He was comfortable, easygoing and relaxed. The main thing I remember about it was my discomfort. I liked him very much—he was very gentle, extremely warm and friendly. I told him that I read his book *Think on These Things,* was very moved by it and intended to participate in as much of his program as I could during the week. He did not follow up on this verbally. Just held both my hands, looked at me eye to eye, and as I recall simply said, "Fine." He wasn't trying to get me to come; there was no encouragement—nothing.

The next thing I remember was a series of talks, interviews, and Q-and-A periods with the faculty and students, which were all filmed. The talks were not particularly well attended. I was there at every one of his presentations. The more I heard, the more I realized that Morrie Schwartz was correct. It's not that I understood everything, but I could grasp enough of his way of putting things—regarding the limitations of thought and knowledge, an emphasis on direct observation and inquiry, encouragement to question and doubt—to be inspired to learn more of this approach to self-discovery.

He started to remind me of my father, only much more at ease. My father also gave me tremendous license to question anything. So I was strangely at home with this beautifully dressed Indian gentleman. I remember his skin impressed me; it was so unlined and youthful. This was 1968; you could figure out his age—he died in 1986.

. . . . .

Q: He was about seventy-two, seventy-three.

A: At the talks, there was a great deal of restlessness in the audience. A few people seemed interested, but there were a lot of long-winded intellectual questions. He answered them thoroughly. I could see that most of us, certainly including myself, didn't really understand what he was talking about. I was enthralled nonetheless.

In addition to the talks, what perhaps had an even greater impact on me was the opportunity to spend time with him alone. This was possible because so few people were really interested. I got to take walks with him. At the time, there were a lot of woods around the campus. I was very drawn to this word *meditation*, though I didn't really know what it meant. I asked Krishnamurti many times to teach me meditation, but he simply smiled and remained silent.

The first time we took a walk, he said, "Would you mind if we just walked in silence, if we don't speak?" I thought that was a strange request. I was certainly accustomed to taking walks with others, but it always included talking as well.

K and I would walk for half an hour, forty-five minutes, an hour—around the campus, in the woods. After the initial awkwardness, I started to actually like it. He was comfortable walking in silence, so I became comfortable as well. It was new to me.

I had walked silently by myself and with close friends before— for example, along the Atlantic ocean and Lake Michigan. However, I barely knew this man.

. . . . .

Q: *What was that experience like? Were you walking along paths? Was he looking up at leaves, walking up to trees? Was he looking up at the sky? Did he stop?*

A: He'd pause sometimes. Sometimes the birds would chirp and he'd stop and say, "Let's listen for a few minutes." So we did. Or he would stop and smile. But he didn't make it a project, like, "Let's stop now, I'm about to teach you meditation the natural way"—he didn't do that. Mostly we just walked and enjoyed moving in silence. Sometimes it was in thickly wooded areas, sometimes it was a path. He seemed very happy. He saw that I enjoyed it and kept returning, so we took such walks on the remaining few days of his visit.

About a day or two before it was time for him to leave Brandeis, on one of the walks, he stopped and said, "Pick out anything. A plant, a leaf, a flower, part of a tree. See if you can look at it for a few minutes without labeling it, naming it, or thinking about it. Simply, with innocence, as if for the first time, just take a look at it. Let's do that for a while." He didn't say how long.

I'm not sure what I picked. I think it was a leaf or a few leaves. At first, my mind got very busy and didn't like doing this, didn't want to simply sustain attention. There was clearly resistance to just looking. I would sneak a peak at Krishnamurti, looking for some sign that we had done this long enough and could start walking again. After a while, though, my mind settled down a bit. I was just watching when, suddenly, the leaf became interesting. I was incredibly moved emotionally, which was totally unanticipated. I started to really see, in a new and vivid way, ordinary aspects of the leaf. Its shape, color, veins, and stem really held my interest. It was all so alive. Green was now really green! There was a whole little world going on.

Then he said, "Well, how was it?" So I said, "It was fascinating. It was just beautiful." And I went on and on about it. I told him how moved I was and how much I saw and how much I learned, that I never was so interested in detail—I had just kind of glossed over nature. Here I got in really close and it was fascinating and moving and it held my interest.

He said, "OK. Now, when you want to meditate, just sit down and do the same thing with your mind." And that was it. [Laughs.] Period. And we resumed the walk.

The other memory I have is every day, there were some professors who went to his talks and discussions—it was a time when professors would meet for cocktails in the faculty club. K always dressed well. When the gathering was informal, he dressed beautifully but informally. When it was cocktail time, it was as if he were in England; he had on a tie, vest, and jacket, like a character who just stepped out of a *Masterpiece Theatre* production.

At the end of the first afternoon talk I recall him saying, "It is four o'clock, isn't it time for your cocktails?" He had a very upper-class

English accent, which I found rather pleasing. I was told he didn't smoke or drink and had been vegetarian his entire life. At the time I knew nothing of his extraordinary life story.

So we went to the faculty club, and the first thing I noticed was how gracefully he fit in. He had some kind of punch—I don't know what he was drinking, but it wasn't alcohol—and he just spoke to different faculty members, most of whom were not there to meet him. Some of the people asked him questions. They had come to a few of the talks. And he would answer, very comfortable and at home with his drink and they with theirs. I do not believe that most or even any of us knew what he was really talking about, but no one seemed to mind.

I was amazed at how he initiated, "Let's go to the faculty club." And then once there, was totally at home. He was completely different than everyone there. Not only was he Indian, but he didn't drink, etcetera. Of course, he was also not a professor, had virtually no formal education.

He had a good sense of humor. Very funny. Very warm. Extraordinarily polite. Really polite! He was a very British gentleman. I've never forgotten.

. . . . .

Q: *Many people who have only a glancing knowledge of Krishnamurti think of him as severe, abstract. Those qualities come across if you just read his talks.*

A: I never found him severe. What I did find, at times, was that he was *austere,* which I appreciated. When he gave talks—all without notes—he was on fire. There was tremendous energy coming through him. He was very, very passionate. And some people interpreted this as being cold. Some as harsh, severe. I would say austere, in the sense of spare, simple, direct—right to the point, and certainly not "diplomatic."

As for abstract, I've never felt him to be abstract. But again, I know his teaching too well. It may seem abstract to some of us, because certain statements that were obvious to him came right out of a great silence, not corresponding with what we know of our inner life just yet. He seemed to be able to infuse ordinary life with that energy, at least in my case, without making me feel distant or uncomfortable.

Once he came down from giving a formal talk, he would sometimes hold my hand, like a loving grandparent; very warm, affectionate, playful, and with a great sense of humor. As I mentioned, he listened carefully. Encouraged you to question anything he said—and he meant it. It wasn't just rhetorical. He wasn't trying to turn me into anything or create a cult.

Despite this, some of the professors behind his back would say, "All right, another one of these Indian *gurus*." In hindsight, this is understandable. Although he often demolished the guru-student relationship, as the week unfolded I did start to look at him with awe. Though he kept mocking such adulation, I was definitely starting to relate to him as a guru. I was inexperienced and starved for a kind of nourishment that the conceptual mind simply was unable to provide. I do believe that after a few years he did finally get through to me. There is no doubt in my mind that he sincerely wanted each one of us to be a "light unto ourselves." I developed immense respect and gratitude for this slender elderly man, while at the same time clearly seeing that he was quite human, with his share of rough edges.

Later on, once when I saw him at the Oak Grove in Ojai, California, he was walking toward where he would give the talk and was dressed in a simple, elegant, sporty outfit—like a Californian. I felt there was something poignant about it. Perhaps in the past, somebody with such profound depth would rarely leave the Himalayas or an ashram or a monastery; instead, the world would come to him, or he'd wander through India. But here was this guy, immaculately dressed, perfect English, traveling all over the world, endlessly teaching, meeting with anyone who would show up and listen.

He always dressed in culturally appropriate ways. When he was in India, he'd wear a kurta and vest. When he was here, he'd wear sports clothes. He had a running suit, a jogging outfit later on with sneakers. He didn't run, he'd walk a lot. He was apparently very athletic as a youth.

I just felt moved by what he was trying to do. It could not have been easy, having to listen to our uninformed, mostly intellectual questions. Normally there's much more of a filtering process going on. You don't go to India and go through all the heat, illness, and cultural adjustment unless you're already pretty far along and/or very romantic about the "wisdom of the East." Krishnamurti was open to everyone and anyone. I noticed that he was very friendly, even affectionate, with the cleaning people as he was with the professors and students. He seemed to make no distinction.

He kept telling us how we could do what he was suggesting: "Don't listen to these gurus, you don't need any help, you can do it, it's all in you." His energy was staggering.

· · · · ·

Q: You talk about his sense of humor. Can you remember it?

A: A lot of his humor was anti-religious stories. Maybe most. There would be jokes. But he also could also be funny—for me—in conversation or dialogue with others. Often a teaching tucked inside a somewhat sarcastic remark.

Once a friend related this story to me. An Indian gentleman questioned him: "Krishnaji, I understand you do yoga every day. Pranayama and yoga every day." Krishnamurti didn't answer, he just listened. And the man said, "This is very good, isn't it? It gives you plenty of energy." Krishnamurti looked up and said, "Yes. More energy, more mischief!"

He would often debunk things. Once you settled on anything, he'd pull the rug out from under you. That was a trait that I experienced and valued throughout.

· · · · ·

Q: I remember you mentioning that he once advised you, in a metaphorical way, to put your house in order.

A: That was when he was leaving and he was packing his suitcase. It was very close to the end of his stay there. He gave a talk which was by invitation only to faculty of the greater Boston area. There were a lot of professors from all over. My memory is quite vivid of this, because it was the last talk he gave before going home, leaving the university. There was a large coffee table, and they set it up so that he could sit cross-legged in his Saville Row suit. Saville Row is custom-tailored, high-class, London. He told me that he had the same clothes for many years, because of never gaining weight.

He was sitting there cross-legged, and they wanted him to talk about education. They gave his talk a title: "The Future of Higher Education." He gave his basic ideas on education: the urgency of self-discovery and understanding to accompany academic learning. Finally, at the end of it, the Brandeis dean of faculty asked a question in a slightly belligerent way: "Mr. Krishnamurti, if what you've said so far is true, how do you see the future of higher education?"

Krishnamurti got very quiet. This I can remember quite vividly; it's as if it is in front of me right now. He got very quiet and said hesitantly, very softly—as if he hated to have to say it—"Frankly, sir, I don't see any future for higher education."

The room of about forty or fifty professors seemed to sink into massive depression—except for myself and possibly a few other teachers. I was dancing with happiness inside; it was vindication of an attitude that was growing within me, presented by Krishnaji with obvious depth and intelligence.

Then I went to his room to say goodbye. He was packing. He let me in on the whole process. I said, "Where do you live, Krishnaji?" By then I was calling him "Krishnaji." He said, "My official home is Ojai, California. But I'm all over the world." He pointed to the suitcase: "This is my home."

He saw how carefully I was watching him pack and he said, "Because I have to pack so much, I've become very, very good at it." He said, "I used to be very scattered about ordinary life things. I had to take that on as a special project. But now, this goes here, that goes there. You fold them neatly. And packing becomes much easier."

I told him my reaction to his talk on university education to the professors. I told a little bit about what I mentioned earlier on—that it's no fault of the university, but I was looking to it to deliver certain things that it couldn't for me. And I now knew that any outer success would be limited in its ability to satisfy me, and that's why I was going in this direction. I told him that when he articulated very clearly what I already had intimations of, it had the effect of enlarging the gulf between the truth of my present condition and the hard-earned and long-held romantic view of "Professor Larry." I was really happy to hear his view of education, because no one in my circle of university friends and colleagues could validate such a conclusion.

Apparently I needed support from someone like Krishnaji, because I lacked confidence. It helped me understand that there was some merit in what experience was teaching me. It was not just an immature, rebellious reaction.

Krishnamurti became very quiet and said, "OK. Look, you are a professor. Do you have any other means of employment?" I said, "Absolutely none." He said, "How about your family?" I said, "No, no. They have no money." So he said, "Do not get into a war with them. They'll win." He said, "There are more of them than you. They're more powerful. It's not going to change right now. Just mind your own business. Work on yourself, but be a professor. Do a good job. Whatever it is you teach, do a good job at that. Do not waste time taking them on, trying to convince them, because it won't work." And then he said, "Put your own house in order. Put your house in order first."

At the time, I had a bachelor's way of life: Throw clothes up in the air and they would remain for a while where they landed. I was very sloppy in my apartment. I said, "Oh, you mean take a look at my apartment, clean it up and put things in order and make sure the dishes get washed, things like that?" He seemed a little bit taken aback. "OK, OK, yes. Of course, you can start there. I'm talking about something else." He just pointed to his heart: inside. I said, "Oh, OK."

Then it was time to go, and I said, "Do you have any parting instructions?" He was going his way, I was going my way. He said, "Just one thing. Pay attention as to how you *actually* live." *Actually.* He emphasized this "actually." How do you *actually* live? Not how you think you live. Not how you should live. But how do you actually live from moment to moment? He said, "The key is in relationship: to people, to nature, to objects, to money. Most of all, to yourself." He said, "People might call that self-knowledge or self-knowing. But pay attention to how you *actually* live." The word "actually" was just burned into my skull when I left. I didn't truly know what it meant until I started to try to do it.

Many years have gone by since that first meeting, which gave my life a new direction. Two years later, I left the university life to wander and learn, mainly from Asian meditation teachers. Ten years in Zen—Korean, Japanese, and Vietnamese styles. Thirty years in vipassana with Thai, Burmese, Sri Lankan, Cambodian, and Indian teachers. For many years now, I have been teaching Buddhist meditation. I even started a center in Cambridge, Massachusetts.

During this time, I saw or met with K as often as I could, mainly in New York and at Ojai. I have also lived intimately with his books, videos, and tape recordings. He helped me change my life for the better and I am reminded of this every day. He continues to help keep me honest from the grave!

What I'm remembering are the lessons learned from personal contact which have stayed with me. His words can be read in a book. I read something of his almost every day and value this kind of learning. But some lessons learned in his presence have been especially transformative—you could say life-changing.

· · · · ·

Q: *In his writings, "what is" is always italicized. There's something very special about that phrase.*

A: The tension between what is and what should be is crucial to understanding him. Although life is lived in *what is,* we seem to prefer thinking our way into *what isn't.* So much of what he says is an attempt to wean us from our powerful preference for what was or what will or should be, so that we can be intimate with our actual experience of what is happening right now. I do my very best to actually live this, and of course it is the core of what I teach. What keeps my life and teaching fresh and alive is this gateway into wisdom.

So now let's go to New York, the last time I saw him alive. He gave talks at the UN, and someone rented a conference-sized room across the street from the UN. It was by invitation. There were about eight of us—a small group, he didn't want new people. Just people who already had a very strong foundation, familiar with his teachings.

We spent a week together. The theme was fear. Two hours every morning, two hours every afternoon, for five days. First, remember, I hadn't seen him in a while. I wasn't at the UN talks. I couldn't get there.

So I hadn't seen him in a year or two, and he walked in and he still had the very beautiful skin and a warm handshake. But I was shocked at how frail and fragile he seemed. He sat down at the end of a conference table, and we went at it on this one theme, exploring it from all directions. Once he started, his body still seemed fragile, but a very powerful energy was clearly there. His stamina for dialogue was always present. He was alert and clear in all our exchanges. It was a superb week.

Finally it was Friday afternoon. The week together was over. There were about ten minutes left before we would all go our separate ways. He was at this point about eighty-eight, perhaps eighty-nine, and he started talking about something that seemed totally off our theme of the week. I remember thinking that perhaps he was suddenly very confused and distracted.

This is a rough paraphrase of what he said: "At lunchtime today, some friends took me to the shop of a world-famous jeweler. I had a very precious jewel in my hand and it was exquisitely beautiful. The color, texture, cut, and the way it reflected light was extraordinary. I held it in my hands for some time, carefully observed and penetrated into—and beyond—it!"

He was holding his hands cupped together. Quickly, with his left hand, he made a gesture as if to throw the jewel out. Then, with his right hand, he made as if to replace the jewel and said, dramatically, "*Fear* is that jewel!" I was stunned, exhilarated and inspired. He had just demonstrated an absolutely central theme in his teaching. And that's the last time I saw him alive.

· · · · ·

Q: *What did he mean? What was he saying?*

A: What do you think it means? Go into it. Find out! I think Krishnaji would be very happy if I ended our chat this way.